ASSESSMENT IN CREATIVE DISCIPLINES: QUANTIFYING AND QUALIFYING THE AESTHETIC

DAVID CHASE
JILL L. FERGUSON
J. JOSEPH HOEY IV

ASSESSMENT IN CREATIVE DISCIPLINES: QUANTIFYING AND QUALIFYING THE AESTHETIC

DAVID CHASE
JILL L. FERGUSON
J. JOSEPH HOEY IV

First published in 2014 in Champaign, Illinois, USA
by Common Ground Publishing LLC
as part of The Learner book series

Copyright © David Chase, Jill L. Ferguson, and J. Joseph IV 2014

All rights reserved. Apart from fair dealing for the purposes of study, research, criticism or review as permitted under the applicable copyright legislation, no part of this book may be reproduced by any process without written permission from the publisher.

Library of Congress Cataloging-in-Publication Data

Chase, David, 1971-
  Assessment in creative disciplines : quantifying and qualifying the aesthetic / David Chase, Jill L. Ferguson, J. Joseph Hoey IV.
    pages cm
  Includes index.
  ISBN 978-1-61229-427-8 (pbk : alk. paper) -- ISBN 978-1-61229-428-5 (pdf)
  1. Creative ability--Study and teaching. 2. Creative thinking--Study and teaching. 3. Arts--Study and teaching. 4. Literature--Study and teaching. 5. Constructivism (Education) 6. Educational tests and measurements I. Ferguson, Jill L. II. Hoey, J. Joseph, IV. III. Title.

 LB1590.5.C44 2014
 371.3--dc23

                          2014002772

Cover credit: Acrylic on canvas, *Jill's Brain...* by Jill L. Ferguson

Table of Contents

Introduction .... **xii**
   Prologue..xii
   Purpose Statement xiii
   Problem Statement xiii
   Overview of the Volume... xv
   Concluding Affirmation...xvii
   References...xviii

Chapter 1: Setting the Context: Creativity and Assessment **1**
   Purposes of Evaluation in the Arts 2
   The Current State of Assessing Artistic Learning 3
   Summary...8
   References...8

Chapter 2: What is Creativity? **11**
   What is Creativity? Definitions in the Literature................................11
   Conceptual Models of Creativity..13
   Componental Theory of Creativity..15
   Investment and Propulsion...15
   Creativity and Learning Assessment 16
   Summary...17
   References...17

Chapter 3: The Connections of Expertise, Practice, and Learning ... **18**
   Domain Expertise and Expert Performance 18
   Deliberate Practice 19
   Constructing Learning 21
   Theories of Learning 22
   Bloom's Taxonomy—Three Domains...22
   Constructivism 27
   Summary...30
   References...31

Chapter 4: Dimensions and Continua of Assessment **33**
   Clarifying the Purposes for Assessment 33
   Clarifying the Scope and Locus of Assessment 34
   Clarifying Assessment through Curriculum Mapping 36
   Planning the Timing and Placement of Assessments..........................37
   Considerations of Subjectivity and Objectivity in Assessment 43
   Summary...43
   References...44

Chapter 5: Models of Assessment in the Arts **45**
   Beginning with the End in Mind 45
   Theories of Learning 47
   Perspectives or Conceptual Lenses for Assessment 48
   Models/Frameworks of Assessment in Art and Design 49

General Assessment Models in Higher Education 49
Theory-driven Assessment Models in Creative Disciplines 51
Structural Models for Assessment Design in Creative Disciplines 54
Summary 57
References 58

Chapter 6: Challenges to Assessing the Aesthetic 61
Challenges with Colleagues 62
Challenges of Structure and Practicality 63
Challenges in Logistics and Consistency 65
Summary 67
References 67

Chapter 7: Where to Start Your Assessment: Technical Foundations 69
Assessment Methods: Fundamentals of Relationships and Pattern Recognition 70
Student Learning Outcomes in a Tasteful Context… 70
Taxonomy of Assessment Methods 72
Using Multiple Methods in Assessment 73
Embedded, Objective, and External Assessment 74
Objective or Standardized Assessments 79
External Assessment 79
Direct Assessment Methods in Creative Disciplines 83
Rubrics 83
Check Sheets 86
Indirect Assessment Methods in Creative Disciplines 86
Survey Research 86
Interviews 87
Southeast Missouri State University, Theatre & Dance Experience Exit Interview for Graduating Seniors 87
Focus Groups 88
Unobtrusive or Passive Methods in Assessment 89
Information from Student Records 89
Information from Agency Files 89
Selecting Assessment Methods 90
Summary 91
References 91

Chapter 8: Online Assessment in Creative Disciplines 94
Online Assessment: Where to Begin 95
Challenges of Implementing Online Assessment Data Management Systems 97
Common Online Assessment Management Systems 99
Deciding on Most Important and Viable Features: What Criteria Should We Use? 100
Questions to Consider: Strategic, Tactical, and Logistical 100
Summary for Online Assessment Management Systems 102
E-Portfolios 103
Other Online Assessment Tools for Institutional Processes 104
Further Resources on e-Assessment 105

References.. 105

Chapter 9: Achieving Assessment Success **108**
    Faculty Involvement in Assessment 108
    Organic Evolution of Assessment—From Individual to Institutional Levels of Inquiry 110
    The Development of Systematic Approaches to Institutional Effectiveness 111
    Support and Resources Needed for Assessment to Flourish 112
    Roadmap to Success 113
    Examples of Developed Plans 116
    Summary 118
    References 118

Chapter 10: Establishing a Value to Art and Assessment and then Explaining Them to Outsiders **120**
    Assigning Value to Art 121
    Assigning Value to the Assessment of Arts 122
    Explaining Arts Assessment to Outsiders 122
    Summary 125
    References 126

Chapter 11: Case Studies **128**
    University of Nevada Las Vegas 128
    Louis Kavouras, Chair, UNLV Department of Dance 128
    College of Fine Arts 128
    Department of Dance 128
    Otis College of Art and Design Assessment Case Study, ... 136
    Debra Ballard 136
    Whole Institution 136
    Introduction 136
    Description of the Problem and Objective 136
    Challenges to Solving the Problem and Reaching the Objective 137
    Strategies, Creative Ways of Solving, and Reaching the Objective 137
    Lessons Learned, Changes Made, and Accomplishments 138
    Conclusion 139
    References 140
    Assessment, Curricular Reform, and Reassessment: University of Cincinnati Case Study 141
    Alexander Christoforidis and Anton Harfmann 141
    University of Cincinnati, School of Architecture and Interior Design (SAID) 141
    Student evaluations by employers informing curricular adjustment over eight years 141
    Introduction 141
    Description of the Problem and Objective 141
    Challenges to Solving the Problem and Reaching the Objective 142
    Strategies, Creative Ways of Solving, and Reaching the Objective 143
    Lessons Learned, Changes Made, and Accomplishments 143
    Conclusion and Summary 145
    University of the Pacific Conservatory of Music 146

Daniel Ebbers, Professor of Voice and Conservatory Faculty Director of
Assessment 146
Assessment Planning for the Conservatory 146
(Professional school within the University of the Pacific) 146
Introduction 146
Description of the Problem and Objective 146
Challenges to Solving the Problem and Reaching the Objective 146
Strategies, Creative Ways of Solving and Reaching the Objective 147
Lessons Learned, Changes Made, and Accomplishments 150
Conclusion and Summary 151

Chapter 12: Where To Go for More Information 152
Conferences 152
Periodicals 154
Articles and Other Writing 155
Assessment Plans, Rubrics and Other Tools 155

Index 157

Acknowledgements

As Hillary Clinton wrote, "It takes a village to raise a child." Planning and implementing effective assessment practices takes an academic village, and writing a book like this also takes a whole host of people from all over the world to serve as examples and references. Thank you to all of our higher educational colleagues who have done research on the topics of creativity and assessment over the last couple of decades, and to those who are just entering the assessment arena and gaining an understanding of how authentic assessment practices improve student learning. We are grateful to our institutions both former and current, our co-workers, our friends, and our family members who supported our vision and understood when we needed space and time to work on this volume. We are also grateful to all of the conferences that have accepted us or invited us to speak about the work contained herein. We look forward to meeting and working with new friends and colleagues as we continue this journey and our creative endeavors. Come visit us at www.assessmentincreativedisciplines.com.

Introduction

We shall not cease from exploration
And the end of all our exploring
Will be to arrive where we started
And know the place for the first time.
— T.S. Eliot

Prologue

When faced with the construction of an assessment volume for architecture; digital design; fashion design; graphic design; interior design; music; fine, visual, and representational arts (henceforth collectively referred to as creative disciplines) in higher education—a work that is essentially consultative and didactic in nature—one is faced with a wide variety of approaches. In putting this volume together, we considered several alternatives:

1. *The storybook approach*: Should we craft the volume to be essentially a story, for example to paraphrase Kipling (1902, 1993), 'Once a time, oh my best beloved, and a very long time ago it was, there was a river of creativity set about with fever trees...?'
2. *The scientific reasoning approach*: Should we frame the volume in terms of mathematical statements, e.g., 'In a controlled and expert environment, let us assume a random variable X such that nonspecific fluctuations in the variable precipitate ideation and inspiration...?'
3. *The sage on a stage approach*: Should we go with the didactic model as in Fux' (1725, 1966) venerable treatise on 16th-Century counterpoint, *Gradus ad Parnassum* – to paraphrase this approach: 'Oh great master, and what would the first step I should take to approach your lofty knowledge of counterpoint', or words to that effect?

In the end, we opted for a practical, down-to-earth approach, one informed by our many years of working with faculty in assessment of creative disciplines. In this volume, we have endeavored to extract the best of what we have learned, observed, and adapted from many quarters. It is our sincere hope that these brief pages will be of practical assistance to faculty, higher education assessment specialists, administrators, instructional designers, accreditors, and others who have a stake in engendering dialogue on educational issues, providing for continued faculty development, and ensuring student success in creative disciplines – a vital part of the fabric of our societies.

Purpose Statement

To advance evidence-based dialogue on assessment in creative and performing arts and design, and to give further voice to the scholarship of assessment in creative disciplines, we decided to put this volume together. Our purposes are not only to provide a set of usable guideposts for assessment in creative disciplines, but also to offer a flexible set of solutions to long-standing issues in art and design assessment – solutions that may be adaptable to a wide variety of specific disciplinary and institutional settings and missions.

Now is a great time for this work to appear. Creative disciplines have been under sustained attack at the policy level for a suggested lack of relevance to higher education and the world of work – but never mind that the MFA is now being referred to as the new MBA (Pink, 2004)! Higher education has generally failed to tell its story in a manner that stakeholders find convincing. This is even more the case with creative disciplines. Without an evidence-based ability to tell the story of our disciplines, our position is substantially weakened and the place of art-making in our colleges and universities is threatened, just as it has been within P-12 education.

New models of higher education are appearing and disappearing with great frequency, yet promising practices are emerging at a rate faster than ever before. Fundamental changes in higher education demand that we adopt those approaches that will advance teaching and learning in creative disciplines - not only to preserve faculty's ability and right to assess student work, but even more to strengthen and deepen practice.

Within academe, deep disagreement and lack of dialogue on assessment in creative disciplines has been the rule rather than the exception. This situation has hindered – perhaps even blocked – meaningful progress until very recently. For example, the first conference on assessment in creative disciplines did not take place until 2009 (SCAD, 2009) whereas mainstream higher education assessment conferences such as the AAHE Assessment Forum date back to the mid-1980s (Wall-Smith, n.d.). We believe that it is time to address the long-standing problems of assessment in creative disciplines. As a necessary first step, we endeavor to bring definition to those problems and to outline briefly how they will be addressed.

Problem Statement

This volume is concerned with assessment in creative disciplines at the college level. To begin with, it is important to understand how we got to where we are now in higher education assessment, but in the end it is far more important to delineate a clear path forward to advance dialogue and practice. The origins and development of the assessment movement in higher education have been well-documented elsewhere. The movement was spurred in particular by assessment reforms in the P-12 sector and pressure on teacher education programs nationwide to provide evidence of appropriate knowledge, skills, abilities and dispositions in candidates for teaching credentials. The movement received decisive impetus through the seminal report *A Nation at Risk: The Imperative For Educational Reform* (1983), through successive iterations of the Higher Education Act, and through the US Department of Education's push to the regional and national accreditation associations to adopt criteria for institutional accreditation – criteria that specifically include assessment of the processes and outcomes of education, not only its inputs. In the higher education arena in particular, quantitative, multi-column spreadsheet-like approaches found early and virtually paradigmatic favor with accreditors and administrators, perhaps best exemplified in the approach first advocated by Nichols (1989). A major disconnect arose in that those disciplines where such an approach was judged by faculty to be inappropriate on multiple levels were largely left out of the discussion, and were left to fend for themselves. Nevertheless, the pressure to assess student learning remained and has only gotten stronger. A central purpose of this volume is to address that substantial disconnect with positive, proven and sustainable practices that can advance our educational practice and our students' learning.

Arts and design disciplines have a natural advantage in terms of outcomes assessment in that student products, performances, and artifacts can be observed, recorded, and visually represented – and thus can be used as a representation of student progress. Equally important to assess, but much less visible, is the interior process by which an artist arrives at a performance or by which s/he produces a design or work of art. We feel strongly that both aspects must be included for an arts and design assessment framework to be of practical value to the disciplines, and therefore devote ample discussion in this volume to utilizing appropriate models for assessment in creative disciplines.

Several problems have proven especially divisive and limiting to the understanding and practice of assessment in creative disciplines, and therefore constitute important themes that are woven into the fabric of this volume. The first issue of consequence concerns questions around the appropriate unit of analysis for assessment. Most higher education schemas rely exclusively on group-level assessment of student learning to ensure norms of validity and reliability (concepts themselves that are an artifact of what we refer to as the scientific method), whereas the tradition in studio-based disciplines is to rely upon individual assessment of student work by one or more artists and educators. This volume treats that unit of analysis issue extensively, and advances a number of practical solutions.

A second problem with assessment in arts and design has to do with the basic philosophy of arts and evaluation of artistic merit – that is the apparent conflict between the romantic view of the artist as being in some sense divinely inspired and the more sociological and anthropological viewpoint of the artist as existing within a set of situations and environments that decisively influence the artist's ability to create. Authors such as Cunliffe (2007) have dealt with this problem at length, and this volume also treats the issue while offering a number of pragmatic suggestions for conducting assessment in a manner that preserves artistic judgment while advancing assessment practice.

A third and very deep problem in assessment has to do with the basis upon which judgments of competency should be rendered, how they should be rendered, and by whom. An unfortunate reaction of the higher education arts and design community to primitive, purely quantitative and 'fill in the box' approaches to assessment was to circle the wagons around the defense of a posture to assessment we might call the 'great artist' theory. Under this notion, only great artists are able to render judgments of artistic merit and competency. While acknowledging the value of having highly-trained and talented individuals assess student competence, this volume offers a broader array of alternatives to traditional assessment that facilitate common dialogue among faculty, students and other stakeholders around student competencies.

Related to the previous problem is a fourth and on its surface an especially troubling issue – that of perceived reductionism of assessment. As creative professionals, we naturally react strongly to any schema that does not allow for the consideration of an artistic, performance or design work as a whole. Adhering blindly to a simple set of learning outcomes without leaving room for the complex interactions of higher order thinking that characterize art making is out of place in assessment models for creative disciplines. This volume therefore features an emphasis on assessment models and methods for arts and design that have been successfully used in the higher education context, including disaggregated approaches that permit more granular, formative feedback, assessment of student works by multiple raters and multiple opportunities that permit such assessment, techniques for engendering evidence-based and meaningful discussion among faculty as to the nature of competencies within a particular creative discipline, and how to arrive and substantial agreement on what constitutes appropriate student competence at each successive level of faculty expectation.

Overview of the Volume

This volume on assessment in creative disciplines is organized around a number of specific topics of interest. Our core themes, the problems of assessment in creative disciplines detailed above, are repeatedly dealt with in context throughout the chapters. While this volume is intended to be read as a continuous work, the authors recognize that it may find more utility as a sourcebook for colleagues who are hard-pressed for time and workable solutions. What follows is a brief overview of each chapter and how it might relate to specific topics of interest.

Chapter One: Setting the Context: Creativity and Assessment – This chapter sets forth the basic principles surrounding learning assessment in the arts. The foundations of theory and practice for effective assessment in creative and performing arts disciplines are introduced, and an overview provided of the core issues and concerns in evaluating and assessing artistic work in an educational context.

Chapter Two: What is Creativity? - This chapter discusses attempts to define creativity from a psychological measurement point of view, and then provides examples of conceptual and theoretical models of creativity. The chapter concludes with a discussion of how an informed understanding of creativity and the creative process can inform learning assessment in the arts.

Chapter Three: The Connections of Expertise, Practice, and Learning - In assessing learning in the creative and performing arts, one size definitely does not fit all. Different kinds of tasks call for different learning strategies, and different learning strategies call for different pedagogical approaches. Students encounter a variety of ways of knowing as they progress through their degree programs. This chapter will explore the connection of assessment strategy to the design and intentionality of teaching and learning through an investigation of learning theory, deliberate practice, and the development of expertise.

Chapter Four: Dimensions and Continua of Assessment - This chapter introduces notions of duration and temporality of assessment; the scope and purposes for assessment, distinguishing between formative and summative purposes for undertaking assessment; considerations of subjectivity and objectivity in assessment; and the variety of perspectives from which assessment can be viewed and an assessment schema or system constructed.

Chapter Five: Models of Assessment in the Arts - The context of this chapter is to clarify those formal and informal models used for assessment in higher education, and to relate those models to assessment practice in design, performing, and representational arts. Of necessity, this chapter also touches on concepts of curriculum, learning design, and learning theory as they relate to formal organization of learning experiences.

Chapter Six: Challenges of Assessing the Aesthetic - This chapter provides an overview of the challenges to assessing the aesthetic and then offers helpful hints about how to overcome those challenges. Challenges include working with CAVEs (Colleagues Against Virtually Everything), overcoming artist egos, getting over the jargon of assessment, how to get everyone to understand what needs to be assessed and why, how to establish value to art and how to get the group to agree on its value (more about this in Chapter Eight).

Just as program notes explain the history and value of a piece of music to the audience and written explanation often accompanies art on display, providing written or digital explanation (text, graphs, charts, spreadsheets) of what was being assessed, how its value was established, and the results of the assessment of creativity is imperative to any reader's or evaluator's understanding.

Chapter Seven: Where to Start Your Assessment: Technical Foundations – This chapter describes authentic, indirect and emerging methods of assessment. We offer a comparative analysis of available methods in terms of their suitability for creative and performing arts, their likelihood of acceptance by faculty, ease of use, and the time, cost and labor likely to be needed. The chapter offers an in-depth exploration of how rubrics may be created and used effectively in creative and performing arts assessment. We provide background on measurement concepts of validity and reliability and their importance in assessment; problems of scalability are also addressed. Finally, we offer a consideration of the multitude of new assessment approaches available through online methods, including unobtrusive data collection, social construction of meaning, and group learning.

Chapter Eight: Online Assessment in Creative Disciplines - While programs in creative disciplines have not been as quick to adapt to the online environment as programs in liberal arts, business, and education, the trend towards established institutions offering online degree programs in creative disciplines is unmistakable. In this chapter we focus on questions of what to assess in the online context and assessment tools that are useful in online environments. Three important limitations to this discussion are that an in-depth analysis of (1) online solutions for tracking and documenting assessment work, (2) e-Portfolio systems available for storing and reviewing student work, and (3) course/learning management systems used as the basic architecture for online courses are all beyond the scope of this section.

Chapter Nine: Achieving Assessment Success – Having a map and a set of guideposts is important in any journey, and the process of putting together an assessment system in the arts is no exception. This chapter integrates concepts of theory and practice and brings together the themes we have discussed in earlier chapters. The chapter includes a discussion of change management, sources of resistance to beginning a program of assessment and other likely bumps in the road. The chapter provides direction and characteristics of what a "developed" assessment system might look like in the creative and performing arts.

Chapter Ten: Establishing and Value to Art and then explaining it to Outsiders - David Hume (1992), Malcolm Budd (1996), and Andrew Ward (1998) have presented various standards and arguments for how to set a value to art based on sentiment, discernment of design, an intrinsic reward system, the inventiveness and/or imaginativeness of the employment of artistic conventions, and the work fulfilling its purpose in the cultural milieu. These ideas will be covered in the first part of this chapter.

Chapter Eleven: Case Students of Assessment in Creative Disciplines – Otis College of Art and Design in Los Angeles, Calif.; University of Nevada Las Vegas's School of Dance; University of Cincinnati's Division of Professional Practice (Architecture); University of the Pacific's Conservatory of Music in Stockton, Calif.

Chapter Twelve: Where to Go for More Information - The last chapter of *Assessment in Creative Disciplines: Quantifying and Qualifying the Aesthetic* provides a list of conferences, periodicals, websites, and further reference materials to help the reader on his/her journey of exploration of ways to quantify and qualify the aesthetic.

Concluding Affirmation

We recognize that a number of long-standing problems have hindered progress on the assessment of student learning in creative disciplines in the college and university context. We sincerely hope that our discussion of those problems and solutions we detail will promote evidence-based dialogue and in the end advance practice. Taken individually, readers may be able to extract information and content appropriate to their immediate needs. Taken collectively, we believe the volume brings together in one place a useful summary of assessment theory and practice that will enable progress in assessment within creative disciplines. We believe strongly in the power and incredible importance of the arts and creativity to our civilizations, our economies, and most of all to the many lives that art raises up, how it enables us to ponder the ineffable, and so become more human in the endeavor.

References

Cunliffe, L. (2007). Using Assessment in Knowledge-Rich Forms of Learning and Creativity to Nurture Self-Regulated Strategic Intelligence. Paper presented at Creativity or Conformity? Building Cultures of Creativity in Higher Education, University of Wales Institute and Higher Education Academy, Cardiff, Wales, January 8-10, 2007.

Fux, Johann. (1725, 1966) *Gradus ad Parnassum, oder, Anführung zur reglemässigen musialischen Composition.* Vienna: Johann Peter van Ghelen, 1725. Reprinted: New York: Broude Bros., 1966.

Kipling, Rudyard (1902, 1993). Just So Stories. Hertfordshire, UK: Wentworth Editions Limited.

National Commission on Excellence in Education (1983). A *Nation at Risk: The Imperative For Educational Reform.* Washington, D.C.: US Department of Education.

Nichols, J. (1989). *Institutional Effectiveness and Outcomes Assessment Implementation on Campus: A Practitioner's Handbook (1st Ed.)* Flemington, NJ: Agathon Press.

Pink, Daniel (2004). *MFA: The New MBA. Breakthrough Ideas for 2004: The HBR List.* Cambridge: Harvard Business Review, February 2004.

Savannah College of Art and Design, (2009). MUSE: Measuring Unique Studies Effectively. Savannah, GA: Author. Retrieved 5/5/2013 from http://www2.scad.edu/events/muse/2009/index.cfm.

Wall-Smith, S. (n.d). A History of Higher Education Assessment. Retrieved 5/5/2013 from http://www.fitchburgstate.edu/offices/academic-offices/office-of-assessment/assessment-tools/office-of-assessment-a-history-of-higher-education-assessment/

Chapter 1: Setting the Context: Creativity and Assessment

Recognizing the need is the primary condition for design.
— Charles Eames

The work of creative artists of all kinds is characterized by two factors present in all they do. The first is preparation and the second is performance. Anyone who has achieved a high degree of skill as an artist has done so through years of work preparing, practicing, and refining their craft; they have assimilated instruction, developed technique, and honed their skills. They have also learned to monitor their own thinking about their work, and learned how to theoretically conceptualize the practice of their art and apply that conceptualization to artistic expression. All of this preparation results in a performance, or the creation of an artistic product representative of the synthesis and integration of all the skills earned in practice. Creative expression is by its very nature an individual enterprise, a lifelong pursuit of the goal of a unique artistic identity. The cycle of 'doing' art, both in practice and product, is the rhythm of life for artists, and is second nature to the way they function.

Analyzing and assessing artistic practice and product, however, can be a difficult task. Evaluating the work of artists and performers is an exercise that is traditionally subjective in nature and has always relied upon the judgment of experts. Teaching and learning in the arts has followed a similar path; the judgment of someone who has mastered the craft is the basis of apprenticeship aspiring artists follow in their development. This model is prevalent today in institutions of higher learning. It is also the case that a vast network of stakeholders in higher education - institutions, accrediting agencies, state and federal government, and the public at large – are sources of increasing demand to know more about how effective educational practices are. It is incumbent upon institutions and the faculty and staff within them to demonstrate that they analyze, document, and understand how students learn and improve over time.

To be truly effective in an educational context, assessment of learning in arts disciplines must employ methods that preserve the primacy of expert evaluation and be situated in a conceptual framework and set of standards that are grounded in the nature of artistic work itself. Such a framework must provide reliable judgment about artistic merit and educational development. Accordingly, an appropriate set of standards must be consistent with evaluation and assessment techniques already in use in arts disciplines, and should ideally provide a basis for understanding student performance on an individual basis and the means to understand aggregate student performance. Methods that assess creative and artistic endeavors should also be recognizable to ways of knowing common in other academic disciplines, and operate in similar terms. This chapter provides a context for how these methods can be developed, and discusses theory and practice for effective learning assessment in creative and performing arts disciplines in higher education.

Purposes of Evaluation in the Arts

Perhaps of greatest benefit to arts assessment is the fact that creative, performing, and visual arts disciplines are fundamentally based in a tradition of preparing students to demonstrate the knowledge and skills they gain as a result of their engagement in the teaching and learning process. The evaluation of performance is central to artistic education. Assessing how well students learn in artistic educational settings can thus provide a particularly rich and distinctive opportunity to understand effective teaching.

Musicians and dancers regularly perform juried examinations, recitals, and ensemble concerts. Visual artists and designers display their works and collect them in portfolios for evaluation. Monitoring intent and execution, self-regulating behavior, and analyzing performance are essential features of learning in the arts, and high order synthesis and integration of knowledge and skill into creative expression is a natural outcome of the process. This is a tremendous strength for arts education to capitalize upon; many other teaching and learning models in higher education are not positioned nearly as well, and practitioners of assessment can struggle to develop a meaningful understanding of how well students are learning.

Despite the abundance of direct evidence of learning, arts disciplines are sometimes hesitant to translate their native evaluative techniques into the language of assessment and engage in systematic analysis of student learning. While identifying outcomes and using criteria to judge student work is common practice in other disciplines, many faculty in the arts are resistant to formalizing what students should know and be able to do into tools and terminology designed for the purposes of assessing learning. Many arts faculty feel that this process tends toward an overly standardized and reductionist way of looking at artistic process and product that is dangerous to the fundamentally interpretive nature of their work: understanding creativity and the individualized nature of artistic expression.

Tension between assuring quality instruction and improving teaching and learning is common in many disciplines. This tension can be particularly prominent in the fine and performing arts. Music, theater, dance, design, and the visual arts all draw upon the application of technique and the demonstration of skill via performance in their pedagogical models, and foreground a highly individual and personalized process of developing artistic voice. In order to relieve the tension surrounding accountability and pedagogy, effective arts assessment should seek improvement in teaching and learning as a primary goal and draw upon methods native to artistic development to meet that goal. Regular student reflection and self-knowledge are essential to artistic development and should play a prominent role in assessing arts-based learning. Understanding the artistic development of the individual, building self-regulative skills, and reinforcing the iterative process of 'doing' art over time are all features that must be incorporated into arts assessment.

Authentic assessment in any disciplinary context is designed to capture direct demonstration of student learning that exemplifies the real work of what professionals in a discipline do. It is a highly effective way to understand learning. Framing an understanding of arts learning in terms consistent with the goals of creativity and artistic expression that are inherent to arts disciplines can provide the conceptual basis for arts assessment systems that have the ability to meet the demands of accountability and the conditions for improving programs and student success.

Developing the necessary components for a systematic approach to assessment in arts disciplines is rooted in the following questions:

- What is creativity, and how are artistically creative learning endeavors assessed? (Chapter 2, 4)
- Why should outcomes-based assessment in arts disciplines be used; what are the advantages and benefits? (Chapters 6, 7, 9)
- How does assessment in arts disciplines differ from assessment in other disciplines? (Chapters 1, 2, 3)
- What organizing principles for assessing student learning in arts disciplines make the most sense? (Chapters 9, 10, 11)
- What does trustworthiness mean in an arts context, and what is its relationship to validity and reliability? (Chapters 1, 8, 10)
- What methodologies are most effective? (Chapters 5, 7, 9)
- What is good assessment data for arts disciplines, and how is it collected, interpreted, and used for improvement? (Chapters 5, 10, 11)
- How can arts assessment address communication and collaboration? (Chapters 5, 8, 9, 10)
- How can learning assessment data in arts disciplines be used to explain effective teaching and learning and establish value to those outside artistic disciplines? (Chapters 3, 9, 10)

The Current State of Assessing Artistic Learning

Assessing student learning in a higher education context serves purposes that seem to be at odds with one another. Some stakeholders stress a need for compliance and quality assurance; others prioritize the improvement of teaching and learning, and some find value in both purposes and attempt to strike a balance between accountability and improvement. It is clear, however, that "assembling and interpreting evidence of what students know and can do as a result of their tertiary educational experience is becoming much more common and may eventually be mandatory" (Kuh & Ewell, 2010, p. 11) as a feature of postsecondary educational operation.

The established body of literature describing the need for and methodology of outcomes-based assessment in higher education describes general principles and provides examples of how to do assessment (Allen, 2004; Diamond, 2008; Suskie, 2009; Walvoord, 1998, 2004). There are also resources designed for use in the classroom to help faculty understand the impact of specific pedagogical strategies on student learning as they are deployed (Angelo & Cross, 1993) and those suggesting effective learning strategies and methods for integrating writing and critical thinking with pedagogy across a variety of disciplines (Bean, 2001). Applied and fine arts, however, have yet to develop similar comprehensive resources.

The tension between quality assurance and improving teaching and learning that is common in many disciplines is particularly prominent in the fine and performing arts. Music, theater, dance, design, and the visual arts all draw upon the application of technique and the demonstration of skill via performance in their pedagogical models, and foreground a highly personalized and individual process of developing artistic voice. The Council of Arts Accrediting Associations (2007) positions achievement and quality in the arts in terms of the work of individuals, and suggests that "Because so much of the source of quality is individual, it is extremely problematic to assume that what works in one case will work automatically in another: 'in pedagogical approaches, there are no universal certainties' (p. 10). Moreover the National Association of Schools of Music argues for policies and practices in learning assessment that preserve disciplinary control with respect to methodology in "...formulating ideas and conditions central to assessment on our own terms... and advocating and defending the validity of our assessment approaches" (Wait & Hope, 2007, p. 17).

Faculty in arts disciplines draw upon a long tradition of teaching and learning that models a 'master-apprentice' scenario where evaluation and assessment are often considered intrinsic to, and embedded in student-teacher interaction (Parkes, 2010). Similarly, conventional wisdom suggests that artists develop pedagogical skill intuitively as they learn their own craft, and formal inquiry into effective teaching is a secondary concern to mastery of performance in graduate programs that produce arts faculty. While this issue is not unique to the arts, there are resources for understanding the learning process in a college teaching context upon which arts disciplines could model to understand and assess learning (Ambrose, Bridges, DiPietro, Lovett, & Morman, 2010; Halpern & Hakel, 2003). There are also resources to assist faculty with outcomes-based assessment (Driscoll & Wood, 2007); for integrating assessment into the regular work of faculty and into the culture of institutions (Banta and Associates, 2002; Weiner, 2009); and for situating assessment work in a context of improving learning and student success and in institutional program review (Blaich & Wise, 2011; Bresciani, 2006). The challenge for arts disciplines is to preserve the autonomy of faculty as experts and maintain individuation as a principle in teaching and learning while working toward transparency in criteria and providing the ability to aggregate student performance to demonstrate curricular effectiveness over time.

Methods that employ quantitative techniques like standardized testing to assess the learning of large numbers of students lack the nuance to which artists are accustomed in their own disciplines, and are not thought to be particularly well suited for understanding the development of the individual in a creative context. Traditional arts evaluation is subjective in nature and relies on the judgment of experts. In order to retain control of their pedagogical models, arts disciplines need to use assessment methods that preserve the primacy of expert evaluation and individual progress while allowing for an understanding of longitudinal improvement of groups of students. Losing this control is the essence of an argument advanced by Samuel Hope, Executive Director of the National Office for Arts Accreditation, who suggests, "the power to decide what must be disclosed can easily become the power to decide what must be done" (Eaton et al., 2005, p. 46).

The use of rubrics for identifying student performance criteria in relation to intended learning outcomes is an established practice, and there are examples of their history, construction, and use in a variety of disciplines (Rhodes, 2010). Sternberg, Penn, and Hawkins (2011) have provided cases studies from a variety of institutions highlighting the use of rubrics, and have also suggested mixed-method and other effective approaches. Rubrics are frequently employed to establish criteria for student performance and their use is widely accepted across many academic departments. Faculty in creative and performing arts disciplines are accustomed to the principles of criteria-driven evaluation and use the technique for admitting students to programs and to evaluate their work throughout a degree program.

There is an emerging body of work suggesting that rubrics and criteria-based assessment methodology can be successfully applied to arts disciplines in ways that are both recognizable to the assessment community and consistent with techniques already familiar and in use by arts faculty. One study has established good internal consistency for a performance assessment rubric used in adjudicating large musical ensembles at Kansas high school festivals, and suggests that adjudicators and directors found useful application for evaluative criteria to improve teaching in comparison to non-rubric forms of evaluation (Latimer, Bregee, & Cohen, 2010). Such an approach has potential in the higher education environment.

Rubrics have also been employed in the evaluation of undergraduate music performance juried examinations, and their use in a study established moderate to high inter-judge and internal reliabilities (Ciorba & Smith, 2009). The authors suggest: "the application of a multidimensional assessment rubric may provide an appropriate means to gauge performance achievement over time" (p. 13). Cunliffe (2008) argues for assessment in creative and performing arts that moves toward a focus on student development of metacognitive skill and self-diagnosis of strengths and weakness in their artistic development, which are essential principles in artistic pedagogy.

Parkes (2010) found that within individual applied music lessons, criteria-based feedback improves the specificity of faculty expectation for student performance. This sort of feedback represents valid and reliable ways to measure what can sometimes be seen as a 'subjective' discipline. Her work suggests that instruction in all arts disciplines can benefit from ideas used in criteria based feedback, including improved communication among faculty, fostering a desire to remove the secretive or subjective nature of assessments, developing willingness to embrace new methodologies, and testing and refining the effectiveness of pedagogical techniques in the teaching and learning setting.

Assessment should focus on three dimensions: the production of good work, the process involved, and development as a person according to de la Harpe et al., (2009) after a review of the literature of faculty publications on educational activity in architecture, art, and design studios and found that the iterative nature of learning and skill development in design studios lends itself to criteria-based feedback, and "assessment of the processes of learning simply requires the students' thoughts be made accessible in a more explicit way than normally happens" (p. 46).

Portfolio-based systems of assessing student learning over time are familiar to arts education, and this model has made the transition to online management and delivery in many disciplines (Cambridge, Cambridge, & Yancey, 2009; Light, Chen, & Ittleson, 2012). Portfolio-based assessment is also effective in inculcating integrative learning in interdisciplinary contexts involving artistic inquiry (Chase & Hatschek, 2010). Regular student reflection and self-assessment are essential to artistic development and should play a prominent role in assessing arts-based learning. Understanding the artistic development of the individual, building metacognitive and self-evaluative skills, and demonstrating the iterative process of 'doing' art over time are all features that can be effectively incorporated into a portfolio-based arts assessment system.

While much of the work of artistic development is individual in nature – one must practice and hone skills over time – it is also the case that collaboration is an essential feature of life in many of the arts. Design work, for example, most often takes place in teams; musicians perform in ensembles large and small, dancers perform in companies. Balance and blend are essential to success. Artists are regularly called upon to communicate in oral, written, and graphic forms, and assessment must attend to collaborative skills.

What remains for an effective arts assessment conceptual framework is methodology that can tie the work of the individual to ways of knowing about aggregate student performance over time. In a review of qualitative methods in higher education learning assessment, Contreras-McGavin and Kezar foreground the value of portfolio-based assessment as a highly effective way to measure student learning (2007). Standardized tests are plagued by shortcomings that render them poorly suited for use to understand artistic development; they "may or may not represent the knowledge or abilities of individual students" (Contreras-McGavin and Kezar, 2007, p. 71). Because the work of an artist resides in direct demonstration of ability, portfolio evaluation is particularly adept at capturing educational progress.

Developing criteria for use in rubrics and using data gathered from student portfolios for assessment purposes requires some familiarity with appropriate evaluative method. In their work on trustworthiness and authenticity in naturalistic evaluation, Lincoln and Guba (1986) identify a set of criteria for qualitative research methodology that parallel standards of rigor from quantitative techniques. These criteria suggest trustworthiness as a standard for naturalistic inquiry, which is to parallel to validity and reliability. This approach is very useful for assessing artistic process and product.

Table 1.1: Positivist and Naturalistic Standards for Rigor.

Positivist standards for rigor	Naturalistic standards for trustworthiness
Internal Validity	Credibility
External Validity	Transferability
Reliability	Dependability
Objectivity	Confirmability

Source: Lincoln and Guba (1986).

Credibility, transferability, dependability, and confirmability lead to authenticity as an epistemological goal in naturalistic inquiry.

Authentic assessment is similarly intended to capture direct demonstration of student learning situated in a disciplinary context that exemplifies the real work of professionals in those disciplines, and it is a highly effective way to understand learning (Driscoll & Wood, 2007). Lincoln and Guba's framing of authenticity in naturalistic inquiry can provide the basis for developing arts-based assessment systems that capitalize on the authentic context of creative performance oriented disciplines. Stake and Munson (2008) make a direct case for the use of qualitative assessment technique in arts education:

> The profession needs to embrace micro-assessment, dialogic practices that link to experiential understanding of what students and artists do; visions embedded in actual teaching and learning in the arts. Researchers and policy makers should stretch arts program assessment in all programs towards qualitative, experiential, contextualized descriptions. That also means giving higher priority to reflective judgment of the quality of programmatic offerings, with emphasis on student performance and productivity" (Stake & Munson, 2008, p. 20)

Using qualitative technique for assessing student work in arts disciplines allows for the sort of interpretation that is central to the work of practicing artists. Work in this area can begin with a focus on identifying and describing quality in an artistic discipline, which is an exercise both familiar and regular to artists and arts educators.

There are difficulties inherent in qualitative assessment, including portfolio-based systems. Contreras-McGavin and Kezar point out that they are context-specific and not always as replicable as surveys or tests, and designing them to meet the needs of all students can be problematic; moreover the process can be labor intensive (2007). These are issues, however, familiar to arts faculty who regularly spend a great deal of time reviewing the work of students on a regular basis in lessons, performances, and studio work, and providing frequent feedback is among the most consistent activities of pedagogy in creative disciplines.

Criteria based practices, common to rubric-driven assessment, can identify the essential skills necessary for artistic development and provide credibility in understanding and assessing learning. Criteria applied to the evaluation of individuals can be adapted to score aggregate student improvement over time, providing dependability and confirmability; transferability is also ensured with the consistent application of criteria and standards. Portfolios are particularly effective for demonstrating change, and as such the dependability and confirmability of improvement over time is a good learner-centered practice that lends itself to aggregation of data on groups of students. While the primary purpose of a portfolio-based system is to understand and assess individual student improvement, there is opportunity for adaptability that maintains the integrity of quality arts pedagogy for the purposes of assessment. It is through the combination of criteria-based and portfolio practices that arts disciplines can develop comprehensive assessment systems that meet the needs of accountability and the conditions for improving student success.

The tension between accountability and improving student success will very likely remain omnipresent in discussions about assessment. Any genuine and truly effective culture of assessment must be rooted in concern for the effectiveness of the teaching and learning enterprise – how do students learn in any given institution? What is the quality of that learning? Learning is what higher education should be held accountable above all else; the strategies, techniques, and results of assessment activity should be carried out in service of quality in teaching and the success of students.

Arts disciplines have always been engaged in a highly effective form of teaching and learning, and much is to be learned from how learning works in the arts. The rest of this book will foreground specific methods and good practices, and serve as a resource to those who practice assessment; it will also assist faculty and students in artistic disciplines advocate for their own models of teaching and learning, and will help inform others and influence good assessment in all disciplines.

Summary

This chapter has provided an overview of assessing learning in fine and performing arts disciplines. Because arts education takes place in authentic settings, the pursuit of artistic knowledge and ability inherently mirrors the most effective learning assessment practices. In order to appropriately reflect the breadth and depth of teaching and learning processes in the arts, assessment methodology that preserves expert evaluation and foregrounds the development of the individual are most useful. Criteria-based feedback and the principles of naturalistic evaluation provide a highly effective framework for analyzing, understanding, and demonstrating learning in the arts.

References

Allen, M. J. (2004). *Assessing academic programs in higher education*. San Francisco: Jossey-Bass.

Ambrose, S.A., Bridges, M.W., DiPietro, M., Lovett, M.C., & Morman, M.K. (2010). *How learning works: Seven research-based principles for smart teaching*. San Francisco: Jossey-Bass.

Angelo & Cross. (1993). *Classroom assessment techniques: A Handbook for college teachers* (2nd ed.). San Francisco: Jossey-Bass.

Banta, T. W., & Associates. (2002). *Building a scholarship of assessment*. San Francisco: Jossey-Bass.

Bean, J. C. (2001). *Engaging ideas: The professor's guide to integrating writing, critical thinking, and active learning in the classroom*. San Francisco: Jossey-Bass.

Blaich, C. F., & Wise, K. S. (2011). *From gathering to using assessment results: Lessons from the Wabash National Study*. (NILOA Occasional Paper No. 8). Urbana, IL: University of Illinois and Indiana University, National Institute of Learning Outcomes Assessment

Bresciani, M. J. (2006). *Outcomes-based academic and co-curricular program review*. Sterling, VA: Stylus.

Cambridge, D., Cambridge, B., & Yancey, K. (2009). *Electronic portfolios 2.0*. Sterling, VA: Stylus.

Chase, D.M. & Hatschek, K. N. (2010). Learning that is greater than the sum of its parts: Efforts to build and sustain an integrative learning model in music management. *Journal of the Music and Entertainment Industry Educators Association, 10*(1), 125-146.

Ciorba, C.R., & Smith, N.Y. (2009). Measurement of instrumental and vocal undergraduate performance juries using a multidimensional assessment rubric. *Journal of Research in Music Education, 57*(1), 5-15.

Contreras-McGavin, M. & Kezar, A.J. (2007). Using qualitative methods to assess student learning in higher education. *New Directions for Institutional Research, 136.* 69-79.

Council of Arts Accrediting Associations. (2007). Achievement and quality: Higher education in the arts. Retrieved from http://www.AQResources.arts-accredit.org

Cunliffe, L. (2008). Using assessment to nurture knowledge-rich creativity. *Innovations in Education and Teaching International, 45*(3), 309-317.

de la Harpe, B., Peterson, J.F., Frankham, N., Zehner, R., Neale, D., Musgrave, E., & McDermott, R. (2009). Assessment focus in studio: What is most prominent in architecture, art, and design? *International Journal of Art & Design, 28*(1), 37-51.

Diamond, R.M. (2008). *Designing and assessing courses and curricula: A practical guide, 3rd ed.* San Francisco: Jossey-Bass.

Driscoll, A., & Wood, S. (2007). *Outcomes-based assessment for learner-centered education*. Sterling, VA: Stylus.

Eaton, J.S., Fryshman, B., Hope, S., Scanlon, S., & Crow, S. (2005). Disclosure and damage: Can accreditation provide one without the other? *Change,* 37 (3), 42-49.

Halpern, D. F., & Hakel, M. D. (2003). Applying the science of learning to the university and beyond: Teaching for long-term retention and transfer. *Change*, July/August, 2-13.

Kuh, G. D., & Ewell, P. T. (2010). The state of learning outcomes assessment in the United States. *Higher Education Management and Policy*, 22(1), 1-20.

Latimer, M.E., Bregee, M.J., & Cohen, M.L. (2010). Reliability and perceived pedagogical utility of a weighted music performance assessment rubric. *Journal of Research in Music Education 58*(2), 168-183.

Lincoln, Y.S. & Guba, E.G. (1986). But is it rigorous? Trustworthiness and authenticity in naturalistic evaluation. *New Directions for Program Evaluation, (30).*

Light, T. P., Chen, H. L., & Ittleson, J. C. (2012*). Documenting learning with ePortfolios: A guide for college instructors*. San Francisco: Jossey-Bass.

Parkes, K.A. (2010). Performance assessment: Lessons from performers. *International Journal of Teaching and Learning in Higher Education, 22*(10), 98-106.

Rhodes, T.L. (Ed.) (2010). *Assessing outcomes and improving achievement: Tips and tools for using rubrics.* Washington, DC: AAC&U

Rhodes, T. (2011) Making learning visible and meaningful through electronic portfolios, *Change*, Jan./Feb. 2011

Stake, R., & Munson, A. (2008). Qualitative assessment of arts education. Arts *Education Policy Review, 109*(6), 13-22.

Sternberg, R.J., Penn, J., & Hawkins, C. (2011). *Assessing college student learning: Evaluating alternative models, using multiple methods.* Washington, DC: AAC&U

Suskie, L. *Assessing Student Learning: A Common Sense Guide* (2nd edition; 2009). San Francisco: Jossey-Bass.

Wait, M. & Hope, S., (2007). Assessment on our own terms. Retrieved from the National Association of Schools of Music website: http://nasm.arts-accredit.org/site/docs/ANNUAL%20MEETING%20PAPERS/NASM_Assessment%20On%20Our%20Own%20Terms-Plain%20Text.pdf

Walvoord, B.E. (2004). *Assessment clear and simple: A practical guide for institutions, departments, and general education.* San Francisco: Jossey-Bass.

Walvoord, B.E. & Anderson, V.J. (1998). *Effective grading: A tool for learning and assessment.* San Francisco, Jossey-Bass.

Weiner, W.F. (2009). Establishing a culture of assessment. *Academe*, 95, 28-32.

Chapter 2: What is Creativity?

Conditions for creativity are to be puzzled; to concentrate; to accept conflict and tension; to be born everyday; to feel a sense of self.
— Erich Fromm

This chapter concerns an assumption so fundamental to performance, design, and representational arts disciplines that it is often taken for granted – that the orientation of these disciplines is inherently calibrated to acts of creation. Creativity is the underpinning of artistic expression, and as such a great deal of the work of educators in the arts is devoted to inculcating it. It is a phenomenon, however, that can be difficult to describe and even more difficult to define. For those who evaluate the work of students in the arts and assess the effectiveness of educational programs, the process of defining creativity and employing a conceptual framework to identify what its components are and how it works is of tremendous benefit. Developing learning outcomes, working with students to explain how creativity works within the context of their program of study, and collecting data from student work for the purposes of assessment are all aided by defining and conceptually framing creativity.

The field of Psychology has a long history of attempts to define creativity, primarily for the purposes of its measurement. A variety of instruments and tests have been developed and employed in an attempt to gauge and score creativity in a standardized way, and numerous research projects, articles, and books have been devoted to the subject. We begin here with an overview of attempts to define creativity and follow with examples of conceptual and theoretical models of creativity. The chapter concludes with a discussion of how an informed understanding of creativity and the creative process can inform learning assessment in the arts.

What is Creativity? Definitions in the Literature

Early stages of research on creativity began at a time when the prevailing thought was that creativity was solely attributable to the predispositions of the individual. It was considered to be a quality of unusual people: those exceptionally intelligent, extraordinarily talented, or otherwise especially gifted. It was believed that "creativity is a quality of the person; most people lack that quality and people who possess the quality different from everyone else, in talent and personality; we must identify, nurture, appreciate, and protect the creatives among us—but, aside from that, there isn't much we can do" (Amabile & Pillemer, 2012, p. 3).

J.P. Guilford and E. Paul Torrance, credited as pioneers in research on creativity (Sternberg, 2006), began to change this predominant view. Guilford, in a 1950 address to the American Psychological Association, called for scholars to probe more deeply. He suggested that individual behavior – especially motivational and temperamental traits, interest, and attitude, interact with cognitive process and a social environment to produce creativity. He further suggested that "It is proper to say that a creative act is an instance of learning, for it represents a change in behavior that is due to stimulation and/or response" (p. 446). Torrance defined creativity as "the process of becoming sensitive to problems, deficiencies, gaps in knowledge, missing elements, disharmonies, and so on; identifying the difficult; searching for solutions, making guesses, or formulating hypotheses and possibly modifying them and retesting them; and finally communicating the results" (1965, p. 663-664).

The emergence of these ideas provided for an understanding that creativity is a complex and multifaceted construct in which a number of cognitive variables relate and interact to develop an aggregated concept of creativity that is recognizable as a process at least as much as an inherent characteristic in individuals. This thinking paved the way to a more sophisticated notion of how creativity operates, and to an ability to analyze a number of discreet factors for their contribution to creative products.

Over time, many who continued the study of creativity began to see creative acts and products not as isolated phenomena, but rather as a process, the result of the interaction of a number of cognitive and affective components (DeHaan, 2009). Richard Snow of Stanford University underscored this process orientation to understanding creativity, and suggested that it is "not a light bulb in the mind, as most cartoons depict it. It is an accomplishment born of intensive study, long reflection, persistence, and interest" (1983, p. 1033).

Having spent a number of years studying creativity, Torrance also observed that creativity had been defined in terms of process, product, and at times personality or environment. He modified his concept of creativity, suggesting that it represents "a successful step into the unknown, getting away from the main track, breaking out of the mold, being open to experience and permitting one thing to lead to another, recombining ideas or seeing new relationships among ideas" (1974).

By conceiving of creativity as a process, psychologists are able to measure any of a number of its facets. Definitions that underscore the action of individuals as they employ creative ability to situations and problems suggest that creativity can be developed. The arts have a long tradition of identifying creative talent and working to enhance it in didactic settings. Techniques and pedagogical methods have been passed from one generation to the next, often through the master-apprentice relationship. And while evaluating the potential one may have for success as an artist is a familiar exercise, developing explicit criteria for assessing student progress over time is often a less common and less frequent occurrence. There are ways, however, that creativity has been contextualized and modeled that can lend structure to assessing student learning.

Conceptual Models of Creativity

While research has demonstrated that attempts to find a singular or unifying definition to creativity continue to evolve and may actually be problematic on many levels, conceptual models have been developed that shed light on specific aspects of the creative process. Many argue that creativity is domain specific (Afolabi, Dionne, & Lewis, 2009); in other words, it must be defined within the context of a specific activity or endeavor. There are five models discussed here that are particularly helpful when contextualized within a particular domain and applied to assessing learning in the arts.

The first is Rhodes' (1961) influential 4Ps model of creativity. In an attempt to synthesize research into a unifying definition of creativity, Rhodes found a great deal of overlap and commonality in what was available at the time. He suggested there are four dimensions, each with its own identity, that together form a conceptual model of creativity existing in what he termed 4P. The 4P model consists of the Creative Person, the Creative Process, and the Creative Product, all of which take place in the context of the Creative Press (Afolabi, Dionne, & Lewis, 2009; Rhodes, 1961). The meaning of each dimension is as follows:

PERSON – identification of the characteristics of the creative person
PROCESS – the components of creativity
PRODUCT - the outcome of creativity
PRESS - the qualities of the environment that nurture creativity

This model provides the opportunity to assess the creativity of individual persons, the processes they go through to create something, the products that are created, and the environment within which a creative work is brought forth.

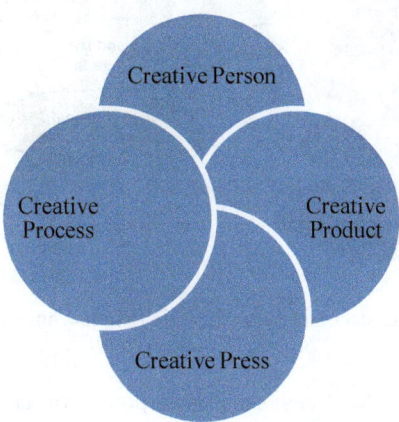

Figure 2.1: 4Ps Model of Creativity.
Source: Adapted from Rhodes (1961).

Paul Kleiman (2008) conducted research with university lecturers across a range of arts, humanities, and science disciplines to identify the qualitatively different ways they think of creativity in relation to their teaching practice and the learning process. From a series of interviews, Kleiman developed five main categories describing how the instructors with whom he spoke conceive of the experience of creativity in learning and teaching. The following themes, and their meaning to instructors, are described as follows:

- Creativity can be a constraint-focused experience where constraints and specific limitations tend to encourage creativity rather than discourage it
- Creativity can be a process-focused experience; there is a creative process through which a work is produced
- Creativity can be a product-focused experience where at some point there is a tangible result
- Creativity can be a transformation-focused experience where the experience frequently transforms those involved in it
- Creativity can be a fulfilment-focused experience (there is an element of fulfilment derived from the production of a creative work

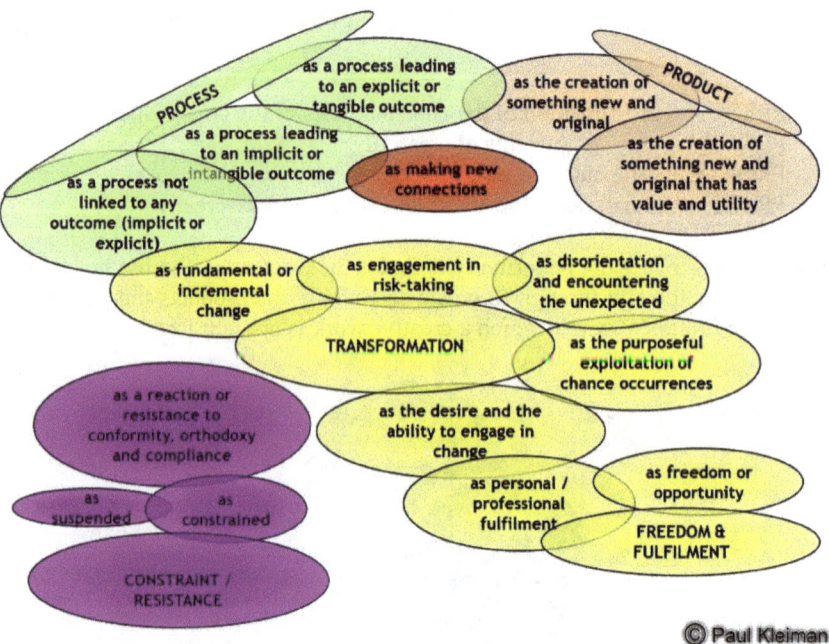

Figure 2.2: Conceptual map of creativity in teaching and learning.
Source: Kleiman (2008).

Kleiman notes that "The transformational power of creativity poses a clear challenge to organisational systems and institutional frameworks that rely, often necessarily, on compliance and constraint, and it also poses a challenge to approaches to learning, teaching and assessment that promote or pander to strategic or surface approaches to learning" (p. 216). Thus for the purposes of assessing learning, systems of assessment need to be sensitive to how different elements of the creative process manifest on an individual basis in the teaching and learning relationship. The process and product for each student in an artistic domain is likely to have goals unique to the individual, and to proceed according to a plan unique to the student and the instructor.

Componential Theory of Creativity

The models of Rhodes and Kleiman account for the elements of the person, the product, and the environment with respect to creativity. Teresa Amabile developed the Componential Theory of Creativity to integrate intrinsic motivation and the social environment with conceptions of cognitive ability and personality in the work of earlier theorists (Amabile & Pillemer, 2012). This highly influential theory includes three intra-individual components that influence creativity and the social environment. The three individual components are:

- Domain-relevant skills (expertise, technical skill, and innate talent in the relevant domain(s) of endeavor)
- Creativity-relevant processes (flexible cognitive style, personality traits such as openness to experience, skill in using creative-thinking heuristics, and persistent work style)
- Intrinsic task motivation

The theory posits that these components combine multiplicatively; no component can be totally absent for some level of creativity to result. Moreover the social environment can influence each and provide training, modeling, and experience. The environment, however, allows for intrinsic motivation, which is an important trait; prior research by Amabile has found that "The intrinsically motivated state is conducive to creativity, whereas the extrinsically motivated state is detrimental" (p. 7).

Domain-relevant skills, creativity-relevant processes, and intrinsic task motivation are very familiar constructs to artists. The addition of influence from the social environment in this model makes it particularly relevant to arts assessment. Each of the intra-individual components contains elements that can be developed into assessable characteristics, as can the influence of the social environment.

Investment and Propulsion

Robert Sternberg, another leading figure in creativity research, has developed two theories that are of significant utility to both understanding the nature of creativity and applying that understanding to artistic endeavors (Sternberg, 2006).

The Investment Theory of Creativity postulates that creativity requires a confluence of six distinct but interrelated resources: intellectual abilities, knowledge, styles of thinking, personality, motivation, and environment.

According to the Propulsion Theory of Creative Contributions, Sternberg's second theoretical contribution (2006), creativity can be of different kinds, depending on how it propels existing ideas forward. The line of reasoning suggests that minor replications to major redirections of thinking are possible, and eight types of creative contributions are divided into three major categories:

- Types of Creativity That Accept Current Paradigms and Attempt to Extend Them
- Types of Creativity That Reject Current Paradigms and Attempt to Replace Them
- A Type of Creativity That Synthesizes Current Paradigms

As with the Componential Theory of Creativity, the theories of Investment and Propulsion can be unpacked for assessable characteristics in a learning context. Each of the six resources of the Investment Theory present opportunities for documenting and understanding learning over time, and the contribution of each can be evaluated in the assessment of artistic products in terms of synthesis and integration. The Propulsion Theory can provide a way to understand student achievement in arts disciplines that stresses originality in creative process and product.

Creativity and Learning Assessment

Finally, it is important to acknowledge the sometimes abstract and ineffable qualities one encounters when attempting to evaluate creativity. Sometimes students demonstrate these qualities (or the lack of them) in a manner so wholly evident to a trained observer that the need to describe and document seems absurd. However, for the purposes of assessing learning, we need to stress the educational process of inculcating and developing creativity as manifest in expression. In this regard, the attributes of skill, originality, and invention that are often applied to creativity must be accompanied by an intentional, well-scaffolded program of intensive study, long reflection, persistence, and purposeful practice. Assessment must attend to that which is developed and then demonstrated in expression. The models of Rhodes, Kleiman, Amibile, and Sternberg are models that are highly instructive for these purposes.

Schools must also be purposeful and intentional in defining the contours of good creative expression, including technique, interpretation, and context. They must also recognize and analyze the social environment they provide with respect to its influence on intrinsic motivation and artistic growth. In terms of Sternberg's propulsion theory, creative arts disciplines are more concerned with accepting, extending, and synthesizing current paradigms as students acquire experience and skill; paradigms are rejected and replaced in later stages of the artistic process, often over the course of a career and long after a student has graduated. The basic questions of learning assessment ask us to consider what students should know and be able to do as a result of their engagement in an educational enterprise. The attempts to define creativity and conceptually model its process and product detailed in this chapter will hopefully augment the already well-developed store of opportunity for authentic assessment in the arts. We can then move to the next set of questions: what are the contours and attributes of good creative expression? How do we know they are present in student work, and what level of quality in that work is sufficient? How does creativity function in collaborative environments, and how can learning assessment attend to communication, teamwork, and ensemble?

Sternberg argues that "creativity is in large part a decision that anyone can make but that few people do make because they find the cost too high. Society can play a role in the development of creativity by increasing the rewards and decreasing the costs" (2006, p. 97). Artists of all types know that cost well and have invested their life's work to a creative endeavor. Perhaps effective assessment in arts disciplines can help to identify the rewards and demonstrate the benefits of a creative life.

Summary

This chapter has explored the connection of creativity to the assessment of artistic practice and product. Attempts to define creativity for research purposes have been elusive and continue to evolve, but those that consider process as a central element in creative activity and focus on the potential to develop and refine creativity provide utility in assessing learning in the arts. The five conceptual models of creativity detailed in this chapter, Rhodes' 4P model, Kleiman's conceptual map of creativity in teaching and learning, Amabile's Componential Theory of Creativity, and Sternberg's theories of investment and propulsion provide examples for how constructs of creativity can be applied to arts assessment. In the educational process, defining and intentionally fostering and developing creativity and identifying it in expression provides a basis for understanding learning over time. Later chapters will provide examples for how the assessment of creativity works within disciplines and how it can be operationalized in models of assessment.

References

Afolabi, M. O., Dionne, S., & Lewis III, H. (2009). Are we there yet? A Reviewof Creativity Methodologies. http://www.cs.cornell.edu/Conferences/ASEE2006/ASEE%20Papers/Session%204/ASEE%20Final%20vs%203_Afolabi.pdf.

Amabile, T.M. & Pillemer, J. (2012). Perspectives on the Social Psychology of Creativity. *The Journal of Creative Behavior, 46*(1), 3-15.

DeHaan, R. L. (2009). Teaching creativity and inventive problem solving in science. *CBE-Life Sciences Education, 8*(3), 172-181.

Guilford J. P. (1950) Creativity. American Psychologist, 5:444–454.

Kleiman, P. (2008). Towards transformation: Conceptions of creativity in higher education. *Innovations in Education and Teaching International, 45*(3), 209-217.

Rhodes, M. (1961). Analysis of Creativity. *Phi Delta Kappan 42*(7), 305–310.

Snow, R.E. (1986). Individual differences and the design of educational programs. *American Psychologist, 41*(10), 1029-1039.

Sternberg, R. J. (2006). The nature of creativity. *Creativity Research Journal, 18*(1), 87-98.

Torrance, E.P. (1965). Scientific views of creativity and factors affecting its growth. *Daedalus, 94*(3), 663-681.

Torrance, E.P. (1976). *Creativity in the Classroom*, National Education Association Publication, Washington, DC.

Chapter 3: The Connections of Expertise, Practice, and Learning

Observe, record, tabulate, communicate. Use your five senses. . . . Learn to see, learn to hear, learn to feel, learn to smell, and know that by practice alone you can become expert.
-William Osler

In assessing learning in the creative and performing arts, one size definitely does not fit all. Different kinds of tasks call for different learning strategies, and different learning strategies call for different pedagogical approaches. Students encounter a variety of ways of knowing and strategies for learning as they progress through their degree programs. This chapter will explore the connection of assessment strategy to the design and intentionality of teaching within programs of study in the arts.

Over the past 25 years, psychologists have developed a deep understanding of the role of deliberate practice in developing expert performance capabilities. The findings both reinforce what many in arts education already know about developing artistic mastery and challenge conventional ideas about teaching and learning. Ultimately, because assessment at its core is inquiry into the teaching and learning process, it is important to understand educational theory and research that can inform good teaching and learning in the arts.

This chapter details the theory, research, and pedagogical practice employed in service of developing higher order learning. The ideas presented here all have particular application to college and university settings where sophisticated synthesis and integration of knowledge and skill are primary objectives.

Domain Expertise and Expert Performance

Because higher education is designed to provide an experience that inculcates complex, high order knowledge and abilities, understanding what is known about the conditions under which expert-level ability is achieved is useful toward identifying and understanding effective in teaching and learning. K.Anders Ericcson, is largely responsible for developing the foundational line of empirical theoretical and applied research on expertise, and is the editor of *The Cambridge*

Handbook of Expertise and Expert Performance (Ericcson, 2006). Ericsson and Charness (1994) describe the conditions under which expert performance is developed and describe how, within a particular domain, expertise is obtained. In the context of this research, a domain is defined as a discrete performance-based activity, such as a performing in a particular sport, playing an instrument, typing, or playing chess. Ericsson and Charness suggest that applying techniques employed in the development of expertise can be found in many kinds of learning and "should be expected in many everyday activities, such as thinking, comprehension, and problem solving" (p. 745). The content and boundaries of an academic discipline are analogous to Ericsson and Charness' characterization of a domain, and as such there is potential for the study of domain expertise to inform teaching and learning in specific disciplines or artistic mediums. There is even stronger relevance to skill development in the arts, where thinking, comprehension, and problem solving are usually accompanied by practice and regular feedback from an instructor.

Deliberate Practice

According to the work of Ericsson and Charness (1994), practicing a skill in a deliberate way over time is central to becoming an expert. While conventional wisdom might suggest that this an obvious and elementary observation, the work of Ericcson and his colleagues has established a sophisticated understanding of developing expertise and the role deliberate practice. In foundational research, Ericsson, Krampe, and Romer (1993) developed the theoretical framework that explains expert performance in terms of lifelong regimens of effortful activities (what is meant by deliberate practice) toward the goal of optimizing improvement. In *The Role of Deliberate Practice in the Acquisition of Expert Performance* Ericcson and his colleagues outline a four-phase process through which expert-level performance is developed. In the first phase, the individual is introduced to the activity and begins instruction and deliberate practice. The second comprises extensive preparation and commitment to pursue the activity full-time. The third, consisting of full-time commitment and work to improve performance, often takes place in a formal setting where the resources are available to develop expert-level ability. This book is aimed at this phase and at institutions where this kind of training is possible. The third phase is the time when it becomes clear if professional career is possible. A fourth phase is also described where students move past the knowledge of their instructors and are in a position to make their own contribution to their field; this is what is known as artistic voice. Phases one through three are characterized by a process of development in which "the individual requires support from external sources, such as parents, teachers, and educational institutions" (Ericcson et al., 1993, p. 369).

This line of research empirically establishes the idea that attributes heretofore ascribed to talent are the result of intense, deliberate practice over the course of time and suggests that approximately ten years of actual time-on-task is requisite in becoming an expert performer; readers may also be familiar with the 10,000 hour number underscored in Malcolm Gladwell's book *Outliers* (2008). The authors "argue that the difference between expert performers and normal adults reflect a life-long period of deliberate effort to improve performance in a specific domain" (p. 400). Moreover they identify the value of this line of inquiry to understanding the most desirable conditions for learning in an educational setting. This body of work has found a significant audience in education and is a major component in understanding the development of expertise in a variety of professions across a wide array of human endeavor. As such, it can be highly useful as an approach to effective pedagogy for teaching and learning in the arts.

In later work, Ericsson (2008) applied the contours of his research on expert performance and deliberate practice to medical practitioners. By this time, a new approach had been established that moved from understanding superior performance on the basis of the opinions and assessment of socially recognized experts to the study of reproducibly superior performance in a laboratory setting. Ericsson described the scientific study of expert performance using examples from chess, typing, and music. He concluded that "complex integrated systems of representation for the execution, monitoring, planning, and analyses of performance" (p. 993) are necessary for superior performance. These systems are predicated on the consistent application of deliberate practice.

It is important to contrast this work with traditional explanations that suggest innate ability is the determinative factor in talent – that the limits of what one can do are established by genetics and inborn characteristics. Research on expertise and deliberate practice has shown, for example, that "problem-solving ability, motivation, and studying strategies... contribute to academic performance, in some cases more than intelligence measures" (Nandagopal & Ericcson, 2012, p. 262) and that "superior problem solving ability in experts for problems within their domain of expertise appears to be mediated by acquired representations that permit reasoning, planning, and monitoring of performance" (p. 263).

There are three central components to applying expert performance theory to pedagogy:

- Identify superior performance using representative tasks that can be captured and reproduced in controlled settings, and discriminate different levels of performance.
- Isolate the components, such as technique, physical adaptations, organized knowledge, or improved cognitive representations that lead to expert performance.
- Trace the development of these components. Describe the cognitive mechanisms and/or physiological adaptations that allow for performance to improve.

Developing a system that attends to these three components is no easy task. Indeed any aesthetic endeavor or product possesses ineffable and seemingly unknowable qualities that make it art, and an attempt to deconstruct that endeavor or product may seem to be folly at best and sacrilege at worst. But, when these components are applied to a process of educational development rather than a judgment of aesthetic merit, the task can become much more realistic. It is important to always consider that "The primary goal of expert performers is to increase the ability to plan, control, and monitor performance by continually improving their mental representations, allowing them to surpass the limits associated with everyday skills" (Nandagopal and Ericcson, 2012, p. 272). A thorough inventory and analysis of the behaviors, successful ideas, specific tasks, and cognitive strategies employed by expert performers is both essential to effective pedagogy and critically important to good learning assessment.

There is also a body of psychological research relevant to practice and expertise that underscores the importance of metacognition, or how one monitors their own learning, as a human ability and discusses its role in being a good pupil. The idea is that metacognition converges with other attributes linked to success in school, and as part of a construct of developing expertise as a student (Sternberg, 1998). In an attempt to integrate the literature on these abilities with the literature on expertise, Sternberg suggests that the two bodies of work may be referring to the same underlying ideas, and that metacognition is indeed part of the concept of developing expertise. Sternberg differs, however, from the work of Ericsson and others in suggesting that deliberate practice in service of developing expertise negates the causality of differences in individuals, rather suggesting that deliberate practice leads to expertise, and that the satisfaction of expertise leads to more deliberate practice. This line of thought is useful in understanding nuances in the literature about expert performance and metacognition, especially with respect to teaching and learning in higher education environments. What is important in pedagogical and assessment contexts is that it is possible to apply techniques used by expert performers, including intentional, deliberate practice, to improve learning.

Constructing Learning

Deliberate practice, domain expertise, and metacognition demonstrate relationships that are important to teaching and learning. Other Instructional theories, ideas, and methods are in use that are effective for learners and can inform and enrich the teaching and learning process. Discovery-based instruction, where learners are not provided with answers and must figure out how to find them, is one such practice. Alfieri, Brooks, Aldrich, and Tenenbaum (2011) distinguish direct instruction, as exemplified by the tradition recitation lecture format, from constructivism, where students are engaged in a context where they must actively participate in the discovery of ideas. Two analyses were conducted in their research: the first compared unassisted discovery learning with more explicit instruction and a second compared enhanced discovery-learning with different sorts of instructional conditions. The findings suggest that unassisted discovery does not benefit learners, whereas feedback, worked examples, scaffolding, and elicited explanations do. Constructivist, discovery-based instruction is conducive to deep learning, requires metacognitive skill of the learner, and is useful in higher order learning skills like synthesis and integration. It relies on the use of authentic tasks in a pedagogical context, and also calls upon engagement in social participation, scaffolding, and the use of tools or mental models to support complex cognitive activity (O'Donnell, 2012).

There are implications here for pedagogy, in that active engagement and regular practice is central to the success of the learner and thus should be central to instructional technique. All of this research establishes a connection among three bodies of literature that relate to effective instruction in higher education: teaching and learning quality assurance, higher education organizational structure, and approaches to learning in higher education. The findings underscore the need for structures that support discovery-based teaching and learning, to which assessment is integrally linked. Before constructivism is explored more deeply, however, it is important to discuss theories of learning more generally, and add Bloom's Taxononomies to the discussion.

Theories of Learning

As part of the conceptual toolkit for putting together appropriate assessment models, contemporary higher education assessment practice has come to include a consideration of learning theories as a basis for departure. Theories of learning can assist faculty in thinking through the assumptions they hold concerning the conditions under which students learn, and in moving from a passive theory in use (Chen, 2005) to an educational model built on our best understanding of the learning process. Learning theories can also aid our understanding of how to facilitate learning in a manner that accommodates individual students – a key aspect in artistic formation within any creative discipline.

Considering learning theory as part of the framework for a well-designed assessment model is crucial. Fortunately, numerous summaries of learning theories are available. Excellent examples include those by Dunn (2002) and Lepi (2012). Briefly, learning theories may be grouped under four major headings: behaviorism, cognitivism, constructivism, and connectivism. Behaviorism concentrates on observable behavior and how that may be altered through instructional stimuli. B.F. Skinner (1968; 1961, with James Holland) is preeminent representative of this school of thought. Cognitivism, represented by authors such as Piaget (1975/1936) and Gagne (1985) deals with how knowledge may be gained, stored, and retrieved through encoding and reworking of cognitive structures, for example through feedback to students. Under constructivism, represented by writers such as Dewey (1938, 1966) and Vygotsky (1962), knowledge is seen as socially constructed. Learners engage in the process of knowledge construction through interaction and collaboration with others. Finally, connectivism speaks to the basis of knowledge as being increasingly external to the learner, distributed within personal and technological networks, changing rapidly, and fundamentally chaotic in nature. From a connectivist standpoint, much learning consists in knowing how to make connections among information sources and how best to leverage those sources within a rapidly evolving knowledge environment. Notable authors include Siemens (2004) and Downes (2007). Learning theories are highly relevant in that a well-designed assessment model might take into account insights from behaviorism, cognitivism, and constructivism, and with the inclusion of insights from connectivism, yielding an appropriate blend of learning theory as a scaffold for learning design and models of assessment within creative disciplines.

Bloom's Taxonomy—Three Domains

Many educators are familiar with the work of Benjamin Bloom (and subsequent revision and expansion) to establish and apply taxonomies of learning objectives to cognitive, affective, and psychomotor developmental domains (Airasian, et al.,

2001). Indeed, the construction of learning outcome statements, couched as they are in action verbs, rely on the taxonomies. The basic structure is outlined in the following table:

Table 3.1: Taxonomies of learning objectives.

Cognitive	Affective	Psychomotor
Knowledge	Receiving	Perception
Comprehension	Responding	Set
Application	Valuing	Guided Response
Analysis	Organizing	Mechanism
Synthesis	Characterizing	Complex Overt Response
Evaluation		Adaptation
		Origination

Source: Adapted from Airasian, et al. (2001).

In each of the domains, development progresses on a trajectory from lesser to greater sophistication such that synthesis/evaluation, characterizing, and origination represent complex constructs incorporating skills from preceding points within the domain. The cognitive domain has been visually represented as such:

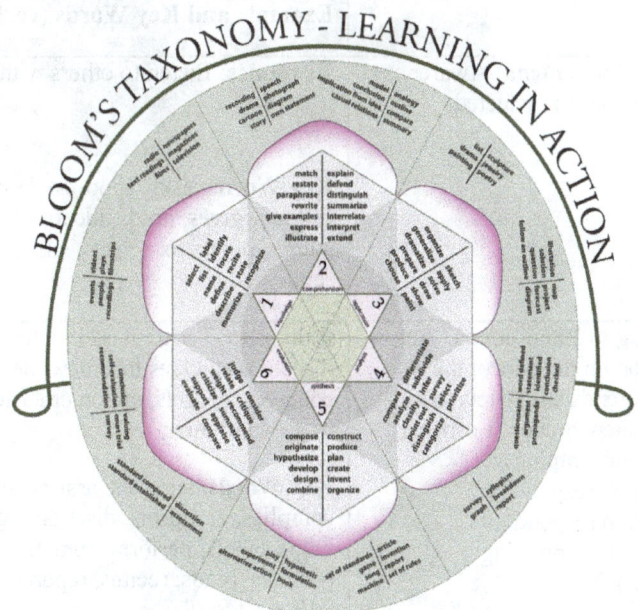

Figure 3.1: Bloom's rose.
Source: Adapted from Kennedy (2008).

Bloom's taxonomy has provided a durable and effective structure for characterizing developmental stages of learning for many years, and it is the basis upon which learning has been understood in all sorts of courses and curricula. Each of the three domains can apply to teaching and learning in any discipline, and because there are significant cognitive, affective, and psychomotor components to learning in the arts the taxonomy provides a useful means of organizing and characterizing skill development. Good assessment of learning in the arts requires knowledge of the learning process, and as such it is important to explore theory in teaching and learning. The most sophisticated constructs in Bloom's taxonomy are attributes shared by highly developed artistic understanding and practice: synthesis, evaluation, characterization, adaptation, and origination.

It is important to note that the affective and psychomotor domains are very important in the arts, but are often not as prominent in assessment literature overall. Many more traditional approaches to assessment draw extensively from the cognitive domain, which for the arts can result in overly formulaic, cognitive-centric outcome statements and assessment practice. We propose a middle path, one that acknowledges the importance of the cognitive domain, but one that also incorporates the implications of the affective and psychomotor domains into the mainstream of assessment practice in creative disciplines.

The affective domain (Krathwohl, Bloom, and Masia, 1973) describes how individuals deal with things emotionally, such as feelings, values, appreciation, enthusiasms, motivations, and attitudes. The five major categories are listed from the simplest behavior to the most complex (Clark, 2004):

Category	Example and Key Words (verbs)
Receiving Phenomena: Awareness, willingness to hear, selected attention.	**Examples**: Listen to others with respect. **Key Words**: asks, chooses, describes, follows, gives, holds, identifies, locates, names, points to, selects, sits, erects, replies, uses.
Responding to Phenomena: Active participation on the part of the learners. Attends and reacts to a particular phenomenon. Learning outcomes may emphasize compliance in responding, willingness to respond, or satisfaction in responding (motivation).	**Examples**: Participates in interactions and discussions. Questions new ideals, concepts, models, etc. in order to fully understand them. **Key Words**: answers, assists, aids, complies, conforms, discusses, greets, helps, labels, performs, practices, presents, reads, recites, reports, selects, tells, writes.

Valuing: The worth or value a person attaches to a particular object, phenomenon, or behavior. This ranges from simple acceptance to the more complex state of commitment. Valuing is based on the internalization of a set of specified values, while clues to these values are expressed in the learner's overt behavior and are often identifiable.	**Examples**: Demonstrates sensitivity towards individual and cultural differences (value diversity). Shows the ability to solve problems. **Key Words**: completes, demonstrates, differentiates, explains, follows, forms, initiates, invites, joins, justifies, proposes, reads, reports, selects, shares, studies, works.
Organization: Organizes values into priorities by contrasting different values, resolving conflicts between them, and creating a unique value system. The emphasis is on comparing, relating, and synthesizing values.	**Examples**: Recognizes the need for balance between freedom and responsible behavior. Accepts responsibility for one's behavior. Explains the role of systematic planning in solving problems. Accepts professional ethical standards. Creates a life plan in harmony with abilities, interests, and beliefs. Prioritizes time effectively to meet the needs of the organization, family, and self. **Key Words**: adheres, alters, arranges, combines, compares, completes, defends, explains, formulates, generalizes, identifies, integrates, modifies, orders, organizes, prepares, relates, synthesizes.
Internalizing values (characterization): Has a value system that controls their behavior. The behavior is pervasive, consistent, predictable, and most importantly, characteristic of the learner. Instructional objectives are concerned with the student's general patterns of adjustment (personal, social, emotional).	**Examples**: Shows self-reliance when working independently. Cooperates in group activities (displays teamwork). Uses an objective approach in problem solving. Displays a professional commitment to ethical practice on a daily basis. Revises judgments and changes behavior in light of new evidence. Values people for what they are, not how they look. **Key Words**: acts, discriminates, displays, influences, listens, modifies, performs, practices, proposes, qualifies, questions, revises, serves, solves, verifies.

Clark (2004); Used with permission from the author

The psychomotor domain (Simpson, 1972) includes physical movement, coordination, and use of the motor-skill. Development of these skills requires practice and is measured in terms of speed, precision, distance, procedures, or techniques in execution. The seven major categories are listed from the simplest behavior to the most complex (Clark, 2004):

Category	*Example and Key Words (verbs)*
Perception (awareness): The ability to use sensory cues to guide motor activity. This ranges from sensory stimulation, through cue selection, to translation.	**Examples**: Detects non-verbal communication cues. Estimates physical proximity of objects and adjusts accordingly. **Key Words**: chooses, describes, detects, differentiates, distinguishes, identifies, isolates, relates, selects.
Set: Readiness to act. It includes mental, physical, and emotional sets. These three sets are dispositions that predetermine a person's response to different situations (sometimes called mindsets).	**Examples**: Knows and acts upon a sequence of steps in a process. Recognize one's abilities and limitations. Shows desire to learn a new process (motivation). NOTE: This subdivision of Psychomotor is closely related with the "Responding to phenomena" subdivision of the Affective domain. **Key Words**: begins, displays, explains, moves, proceeds, reacts, shows, states, volunteers.
Guided Response: The early stages in learning a complex skill that includes imitation and trial and error. Adequacy of performance is achieved by practicing.	**Examples**: Performs a skill or technique as demonstrated. Follows instructions. Responds to instructive signals. **Key Words**: copies, traces, follows, react, reproduce, responds
Mechanism (basic proficiency): This is the intermediate stage in learning a complex skill. Learned responses have become habitual and the movements can be performed with some confidence and proficiency.	**Examples**: Execute technique. **Key Words**: assembles, calibrates, constructs, dismantles, displays, fastens, fixes, grinds, heats, manipulates, measures, mends, mixes, organizes, sketches.

Complex Overt Response (Expert): The skillful performance of motor acts that involve complex movement patterns. Proficiency is indicated by a quick, accurate, and highly coordinated performance, requiring a minimum of energy. This category includes performing without hesitation, and automatic performance.	**Examples**: Maneuvers a car into a tight parallel parking spot. Operates a computer quickly and accurately. Displays competence while playing the piano. **Key Words**: assembles, builds, calibrates, constructs, dismantles, displays, fastens, fixes, grinds, heats, manipulates, measures, mends, mixes, organizes, sketches. NOTE: The Key Words are the same as Mechanism, but will have adverbs or adjectives that indicate that the performance is quicker, better, more accurate, etc.
Adaptation: Skills are well developed and the individual can modify movement patterns to fit special requirements.	**Examples**: Responds effectively to unexpected experiences. Modifies instruction to meet the needs of the learners. **Key Words**: adapts, alters, changes, rearranges, reorganizes, revises, varies.
Origination: Creating new movement patterns to fit a particular situation or specific problem. Learning outcomes emphasize creativity based upon highly developed skills.	**Examples**: Composes or develops aesthetic interpretation with artistic voice. **Key Words**: arranges, builds, combines, composes, constructs, creates, designs, initiate, makes, originates.

Clark (2004); Used with permission from the author

Deliberate practice in service of expert performance leads this sort of development, and getting there is a process of constructive learning.

Constructivism

Earlier in this chapter, we discussed theories of learning and how they connect to pedagogy. One of those theories – constructivism – is critical to arts education and models of assessing artistic learning. Many educational scholars suggest that learners construct knowledge in large measure through interaction and assimilation with previous experience, and this notion is woven into a number of threads in the theory of what has come to be called constructivism. Dewey, Piaget, and Vygotsky are among those who have developed a range of educational theory generated from this concept (O'Donnell, 2012), and while there is no unified theoretical framework or definition for constructivism, the "relative role of the individual and context in which the individual is embedded" is at its core, and "key characteristics of constructivist learning environments include the important role of community in learning environments, the use of authentic tasks, and the use of tools (broadly defined) to support learning" (O'Donnell, 2012, p. 61).

David Moshman (1982) distinguished three forms of constructivism, each of which correlate to instructional approaches. They are:

> **Exogenous Constructivism** – Knowledge is derived from the environment. The traditional lecture-recitation format is based in exogenous constructivism.
>
> **Endogenous Constructivism** – As illustrated by the theory of Piaget, who described cognitive development as occurring through a process of adaptation, which itself consists of the subprocesses of assimilation and accommodation. The learner constructs new knowledge by means of adapting existing knowledge through assimilation and accommodation with knowledge they already possess. Teaching is designed to challenge the learner to draw upon internal resources to develop new strategies for learning.
>
> **Dialectical Constructivism** – Knowledge lies in the continual interaction between the individual and the environment. Context matters greatly. Learning is predicated on the relationship of the individual to an environment. Instructors provide models, which are then practiced and internalized by the learner. The teacher explains, corrects, and asks the student to explain, scaffolding the work of the learner in order to develop knowledge and skill.

The principles of constructivism are native to the learning environment in most arts disciplines, especially those of endogenous and dialectical constructivism. The dialectical model is particularly significant, and deserves greater elaboration. It emphasizes five elements:

> **Social participation**. Learners develop competence, and new knowledge is integrated with existing knowledge in an environment of shared values and meaning-making.
>
> **Scaffolding**. The learner is guided through a structured system of support, ideally one in which support changes character and diminishes as the learner demonstrates increasing ability. The instructor provides regular and detailed feedback that similarly fades as appropriate through the developmental process, channeling and focusing the performance of the student and modeling as necessary (Pea, 2004).
>
> **Authentic tasks**. The tasks in which learners engage are situated in meaningful experiences directly demonstrative of the real-word tasks that educational exercises are designed to emulate.

Tools that support learning. The environment in which learning occurs fosters strategies and interaction that result in the creation of artifacts and products (tools) that mediate development.

The dialectic between the individual and the environment. Instructors provide support through asking increasingly complex questions and requiring increasingly sophisticated demonstration of learning as a shared understanding between the teacher and learner is developed. The observation of and interaction with more advanced students also contributed to this dialectic.

Adapted from O'Donnell (2012)

Arts educators are inherently familiar with the dialectical constructivist model of learning. Social participation is as essential a feature, for example, in the studio and in individual instruction as it is in ensemble performances and exhibits. Scaffolding enables formative assessment, and both formative and summative assessments revolve around authentic tasks. The tools that support learning are the artistic products themselves – sometimes artifacts and sometimes performance according to medium and discipline. And the dialectic between the individual and the environment is a constant feature of learning in the arts, in formal and informal settings where students engage and interact with instructors, artistic products, and each other.

Scaffolding also deserves special attention, as it is so often an integral method in teaching artists. It is dependent upon instructional planning and delivery that leads the student from what they already know and can do to more advanced knowledge and ability, with support from the instructor throughout the process (Lipscomb, Swanson, & West, 2004; O'Donnell, 2012). There are five features involved in effective scaffolding:

1. **Intentionality**. Instruction should link cognition and performance to help the student successfully complete learning objectives.
2. **Appropriateness**. The objective should be sufficiently difficult to challenge the student and require assistance from the instructor.
3. **Modeling**. The instructor models learning strategies and skills and demonstrated and questions in a manner appropriate for illustration of these strategies and skills.
4. **Partnering**. The relationship of teacher and student is that of partnership in a common endeavor in which the student is a colleague (albeit less experienced and accomplished) of the instructor.
5. **Fading support**. The teacher gradually diminishes support as the student demonstrates appropriate development.

(Applebee and Langer, 1983)

The key components of dialectical constructivism and scaffolding are outlined in this table:

Table 3.2: Dialectical constructivism and learning environment attributes.

Element of Dialectical Constructivism	Attributes in the Learning Environment
SOCIAL PARTICIPATION	Provide an environment fostering shared values and participatory meaning-making
SCAFFOLDING	Lead students from what they already know to a deep understanding of new material; provide instructional support at each step
SCAFFOLDING 1: Intentionality	Each instructional activity contributes to helping the learner complete the task
SCAFFOLDING 2: Appropriateness	The task must be sufficiently difficult for the learner to require assistance
SCAFFOLDING 3: Modeling	The instructor models task-related strategies and asks questions that illustrate appropriate strategies for approaching the task
SCAFFOLDING 4: Instructional Relationship	The instructor and student are partners. The teacher invites learner's efforts and redirects the learner's strategies when necessary and appropriate
SCAFFOLDING 5: Diminishing Support	The instructor diminishes support when the learner can perform the task alone
AUTHENTIC TASKS	Educational tasks mirror real-world situations
TOOLS TO SUPPORT LEARNING	Performances and artistic products are a central feature of the learning environment
INDIVIDUAL AND SOCIAL ENVIRONMENT	Instruction moves from lesser to greater complexity; demonstration of learning is expected to become more sophisticated

The principles of constructivism, including the importance of the educational environment, social engagement, scaffolding, adaptation, increasing complexity over time, and individual development predicated on close instructional interaction are not new to artists. The master-apprentice model was essentially constructivist long before the theory was enshrined into educational theory. Its principles are embedded in pedagogy in the arts, and as such they are essential and foundational to arts assessment.

Summary

Understanding how deliberate practice, expert performance, and learning theory impact educational development in creative and artistic disciplines can provide benefit and utility toward developing good teaching that results in good learning. A balanced approach to understanding the interaction of cognitive, affective and psychomotor domains with reference to Bloom's taxonomy can be applied to learning outcomes in a more effective way when viewed through the lens of constructivism, and carefully crafted, intentional scaffolding of student development can be an excellent dimension and point of focus for evaluation of student work and broader curricular assessment on both individual and collective levels.

References

Airasian, P. W., Cruikshank, K. A., Mayer, R. E., Pintrich, P. R., Wittrock, J. R. M. C., Andersonand, L. W., & Krathwohl, D. R. (2001). A Taxonomy for Learning, Teaching, and Assessing: A Revision of Bloom's Taxonomy of Educational Objectives. *New York: Addison Wesley Longmann.*

Applebee, A.N., & Langer, J. (1983). Instructional scaffolding: Reading and writing as natural language activities. *Language Arts, 60*, 168-175.

Clark, D. (2004). *Concepts of leadership.* Retrieved from http://nwlink.com/~donclark/leader/leadcon.html

Dewey, John. (1938). *Experience and Education.* New York: Macmillan.

Dewey, John. (1966). *Democracy and Education.* New York: Free Press.

Downes, S. (2005). An Introduction to Connective Knowledge. in Hug, Theo (ed.) (2007): Media, Knowledge & Education - Exploring new Spaces, Relations and Dynamics in Digital Media Ecologies. Proceedings of the International Conference held on June 25-26, 2007. November 27, 2007.

Dunn, L. (2002). *Theories of Learning.* Oxford: Oxford Brookes University Centre for Staff and Learning Development. Retrieved January 2, 2013 from http://www.brookes.ac.uk/services/ocsld/resources/briefing_papers/learning_theories.pdf.

Ericsson, K. A., Krampe, R. T., & Tesch-Römer, C. (1993). The role of deliberate practice in the acquisition of expert performance. *Psychological Review, 100*(3), 363.

Ericsson, K. A. (Ed.). (2006). The Cambridge handbook of expertise and expert performance. Cambridge University Press.

Ericsson, K.A. (2008). Deliberate practice and acquisition of expert performance: A general overview. *Academic Emergency Medicine, 15*(11), 988-994. doi: 10.1111/j.1553-2712.2008.00227.x

Ericsson, K. A., & Charness, N. (1994). Expert performance: Its structure and acquisition. *American Psychologist, 49*(8), 725-747. doi: 10.1037/0003-066X.49.8.725

Gagne, R. (1985). The Conditions of Learning (4th ed). New York: Holt, Rinehart & Winston

Gladwell, M. (2008). *Outliers: The story of success.* Little, Brown and Company, New York, NY.

Krathwohl, D. R., Bloom, B. S., & Masia, B. B. (1973). *Taxonomy of Educational Objectives, the Classification of Educational Goals. Handbook II: Affective Domain.* New York: David McKay Co., Inc.

Moshman, D. (1982). Exogenous, endogenous, and dialectical constructivism. *Developmental Review*, 2, 371-384. Doi: 10.1016/0273-2297(82)90019-3.

Nandagopal, Kiruthiga; Ericsson, K. Anders (2012). Enhancing students' performance in traditional education: Implications from the expert performance approach and deliberate practice. Harris, Karen R. (Ed); Graham, Steve (Ed); Urdan, Tim (Ed); McCormick, Christine B. (Ed); Sinatra, Gale M. (Ed); Sweller, John (Ed). *APA educational psychology handbook, Vol 1: Theories, constructs, and critical issues.* (pp. 257-293). Washington, DC, US: American Psychological Association, xxx, 621 pp. doi: 10.1037/13273-010

O'Donnell, A. M. (2012). Constructivism. Harris, Karen R. (Ed); Graham, Steve (Ed); Urdan, Tim (Ed); McCormick, Christine B. (Ed); Sinatra, Gale M. (Ed); Sweller, John (Ed), (2012). APA educational psychology handbook, Vol 1: Theories, constructs, and critical issues. , (pp. 61-84). Washington, DC, US: American Psychological Association, xxx, 621 pp. doi: 10.1037/13273-003

Lepi, Katie (2012). A Simple Guide to 4 Complex Learning Theories. *Edudemic*, Monday, December 24, 2012. Retrieved from http://edudemic.com/2012/12/a-simple-guide-to-4-complex-learning-theories on January 2, 2013.

Lipscom, L., Swanson, J., & West, A. (2004) Scaffolding. In M. Orey (ed.) *Emerging perspectives on leaning, teaching, and technology*. Retrieved from http://projects.coe .uga/epltt/index.php?title=Scaffolding.

Pea, R. (2004). The social and technological dimensions of scaffolding and related theoretical concepts for learning, education, and human activity. *Journal of the Learning Sciences, 13*, 423-451. doi: 10.1207/s15327809jls1303_6.

Piaget, J (1975/1936). *La naissance de l'intelligence chez l'enfant. [Emergence of intelligence in the child] in Three theories of cognitive representation and their evaluation standards of training effect*. Neuchatel: Delachaux et Nieslé/Heerlson, The Netherlands: Heerlson.

Siemens, G. (2004, updated 2005). Connectivism: A Learning Theory for the Digital Age. Retrieved January 2, 2013 from
http://www.elearnspace.org/Articles/connectivism.htm .

Simpson E. J. (1972). *The Classification of Educational Objectives in the Psychomotor Domain.* Washington, DC: Gryphon House.

Skinner, B., *The Technology of Teaching*, 1968. New York: Appleton-Century-Crofts.

Sternberg, R. J. (1998). Metacognition, abilities, and developing expertise: What makes an expert student? *Instructional Science, 26*(1), 127-140.

Vygotsky, D. (1962). *Thought and language.* Cambridge, MA: MIT Press.

Chapter 4: Dimensions and Continua of Assessment

Evolution is not a force but a process; not a cause but a law.
– John, Viscount of Blackburn

This chapter introduces notions of the scope and purposes for assessment, duration and temporality of assessment, distinguishing between formative and summative purposes for undertaking assessment; considerations of subjectivity and objectivity in assessment; and the variety of perspectives from which assessment can be viewed and an assessment schema or system constructed.

Clarifying the Purposes for Assessment

The introductory chapter to this volume outlines a number of tensions that have limited the understanding and practice of student learning outcomes assessment in creative disciplines. One of those tensions concerns the distinction frequently made between assessment and evaluation, the former being thought of as generally undertaken for ongoing (formative) improvement of teaching and learning, and the latter being thought of as an overall (summative) judgment of merit or worth. The formative vs. summative distinction was first described by Scriven (1967) and has been in wide use since that time. According to the National Academy for Academic Leadership (n.d.), the concepts of assessment and evaluation may be understood best in comparison to one another:

> **Assessment** is a process of determining "what is." Assessment provides faculty members, administrators, trustees, and others with evidence, numerical or otherwise, from which they can develop useful information about their students, institutions, programs, and courses and also about themselves. This information can help them make effectual decisions about student learning and development, professional effectiveness, and program quality. **Evaluation** uses information based on the credible

evidence generated through assessment to make judgments of relative value: the acceptability of the conditions described through assessment.[1]

Another way to think about the distinctions between assessment and evaluation is to compare them across dimensions of (1) Content, timing, and purpose; (2) Orientation, or focus of measurement, and (3) Findings, in terms of how results are used.

Table 4.1: Differences between assessment and evaluation.

Dimensions of Difference	Assessment	Evaluation
Content: Timing, primary purpose	**Formative**: Ongoing, to improve learning	**Summative**: Final, to gauge quality
Orientation: Focus of measurement	**Process-oriented**: How learning is proceeding	**Product-oriented**: What has been learned
Findings: uses of information and results	**Diagnostic**: Identify areas for improvement	**Judgmental**: Arrive at an overall grade/score/estimate of worth

Note: Adapted from Duke University, Academic Resource Center (n.d.).

Understanding the distinction between assessment and evaluation is vital, since the ongoing improvement of student learning, instructional strategies and methods that contribute to such improvement is the basic standpoint of assessment to which good practice adheres, as thoughtfully articulated in the AAHE *Principles of Good Practice in Student Learning* (1991).

The assessment vs. evaluation waters get muddied when accountability demands of state and federal agencies, essentially summative evaluation, are taken to be one and the same as formative assessment. Furthermore, over the last three decades regional, national, and specialized accreditation agencies have, as a condition of their re-approval by the U.S. Department of Education, adopted accreditation criteria that effectively mandate the development of formative assessment systems within programs, schools, and institutions. On the negative side, this top-down imposition of criteria and workload did not receive an overwhelmingly positive reception from the academy and has taken root slowly. On the positive side, the impetus for change coupled with the necessity of continued accreditation and eligibility for federal financial aid programs has no doubt accelerated the natural development in our understanding of the teaching and learning process.

Clarifying the Scope and Locus of Assessment

The locus of assessment and basis for analysis are areas that, if not appropriately clarified, can result in fundamental misunderstandings, frustration, and lack of communication – another problem alluded to in the introductory chapter of this volume. Not only do multiple genres of assessment methods exist, but they also find application in one or more of the multiple loci for assessment in creative disciplines:

---

[1] Source: http://www.thenationalacademy.org/readings/assessandeval.html.

- Individual student assessment, for which we will need individualized student learning outcomes;
- Assessment of multiple students at the course or studio level, for which we need course-level or studio-level student learning outcomes;
- Program-level assessment, requiring program-level student learning outcomes, and finally
- Assessment at the institutional level, requiring institution-level student learning outcomes – usually stated broadly, at a high level of abstraction.

Table 4.2: Multiple loci for assessment.

Unit of Analysis	Basis for Assessment	Who or what body is most likely to undertake assessment	Scope of decisions: how assessment is used
Individual student assessment	Individual student learning outcomes	Individual faculty member	Individual artistic mentoring and guiding; comparison of individual student growth over time
Multiple students in a studio or section: course-level assessment	Course-level student learning outcomes	Individual faculty member; multiple raters for student projects	Adjustments in course content, assignments, and sequencing to aid student learning; adjustments or refinements to faculty expectations for student learning within the course
Students in a degree program: program-level assessment	Program-level student learning outcomes	Multiple faculty members within a department, and external raters for experiential learning projects	Adjustments and changes in course content within the curriculum; sequencing of curriculum; changes in key assignments within core courses in the curriculum; adjustments or refinements to faculty expectations for student learning within the degree program

Students within a school, college or university: institution-level assessment	Institution-level student learning outcomes	Faculty within a school, college or university assessment committee, institutional effectiveness committee, or curriculum committee	Adjustments and changes in course content within general education; sequencing of the curriculum; changes in key assignments within general education courses; adjustments or refinements to faculty expectations for student learning within general education courses.

Many schools of art, music, design, drama, and other creative disciplines exist within larger colleges or universities. In those instances, general education or breadth learning outcomes that are important at the institutional level (and in the United States are mandated by regional accreditors) must also form part of the assessment schema. As determined through collective faculty determination at each institution, student learning outcomes relevant to general education might include critical thinking/metacognitive skills, reading and writing, ethical development, information literacy, and quantitative reasoning, among others.

Clarifying Assessment through Curriculum Mapping

It aids our collective understanding of what we want our students to learn if we chart out our assessment schema. We should first tabulate the relationships among and between course-level, program-level, and institution-level student learning outcomes. Doing such a mapping exercise, faculty frequently find areas of overlap as well as expected areas of achievement that are not well-addressed and will need to be bolstered. An example of a curriculum map for a Bachelor of Arts in Jazz Studies from the University of the Pacific is appended below. For each of the program-level student learning outcomes, the curriculum map indicates the extent to which each required course introduces, reinforces, or requires mastery of that student learning outcome within the context of the course.

Map of Jazz Studies, B.A.

	Facility	Improvisation	Composing/Arranging	Knowledge
	Recognize, identify, and demonstrate analytical and performance facility in major jazz idioms.	Improvisation—Integrate theoretical understanding of harmony, melody, form, structure, and chord/scale relationships with performance and fluency in the jazz language.	Composition/Arranging—Create original compositions and develop experience arranging original and standard literature for small groups and big bands.	Knowledge of Jazz history and literature—Incorporate knowledge of jazz history and literature, as well as the cultural sources and influences of jazz into analysis, composition/arranging, and performance.
Intro to Jazz	N/A	N/A	N/A	Introduced
Jazz Piano I	N/A	Introduced	N/A	N/A
Jazz Piano II	N/A	Developed	N/A	N/A
Jazz Theory & Aural Training	Introduced	Introduced	N/A	N/A
Jazz Style & Analysis	Developed	Developed	N/A	N/A
Jazz Improvisation I	N/A	Introduced	N/A	N/A
Jazz Improvisation II	N/A	Developed	N/A	N/A
Advanced Improvisation	N/A	Mastered	N/A	N/A
Jazz Ensemble	N/A	Developed	N/A	Developed
Jazz Combo	N/A	Developed	N/A	Developed
Jazz Composition & Arranging	N/A	N/A	Developed	N/A
Jazz Pedagogy	N/A	N/A	N/A	Introduceed
Advanced History of Jazz	N/A	N/A	N/A	Developed
Jazz Seminar & Perspectives I	N/A	Developed	N/A	Developed
Jazz Seminar & Perspectives II	N/A	Developed	N/A	Developed
Jazz Seminar & Perspectives III	N/A	Developed	N/A	Developed
Jazz Seminar & Perspectives IV	N/A	Mastered	N/A	Mastered
Jazz Applied I	Introduced	Introduced	N/A	N/A
Jazz Applied II	Developed	Developed	N/A	N/A
Jazz Applied III	Developed	Developed	N/A	N/A
Jazz Applied IV	Mastered	Mastered	N/A	N/A

Figure 4.1: Curriculum map of Jazz Studies
Source: University of the Pacific (n.d.)
Note: Used by permission.

Planning the Timing and Placement of Assessments

Next, we should chart out those assessment tools, timings, and opportunities by discipline that go in to our assessment schema. A good assessment schema in creative disciplines needs to be appropriate to the point in a course of study at which it is used and the level of accomplishment expected. There are points within the course of study that are more appropriate for some assessment methods than for others, thus temporality is an important consideration in selecting assessment methods. Deciding when and where to use various assessments in a program of study is an important collective faculty decision. Many programs utilize assessments of signature assignments within courses in the major to act as expected milestones for student learning; performing arts programs utilize periodic juries and end of term performances to obtain in-process assessments, and senior recitals for capstone assessment of student competencies. In the representational arts and design programs, portfolios serve the same function. Ewell (1984) advised academic programs to utilize for assessment those points of contact where the student encounters a program milestone, usually one that includes interface with the program or college administrative system in some form.

The table below provides a generic example of what a completed plan for the timing and placement of various assessments might be, and how various assessment methods can be utilized appropriately at different points in time throughout the degree program of study or student life cycle. Four common program-level student learning outcomes at the undergraduate level are provided as a basis for comparing assessment methods that may be appropriate and in what situations they should be used:

- Acquisition of knowledge, skills, and abilities in the discipline
- Achievement of program-level student learning outcomes
- Growth in metacognitive skills and self-reflective abilities
- Preparation for professional practice

Of necessity, the guide below is limited and creative colleagues will need to expand it to better suit their own purposes and the specifics of their programs of study.

DIMENSIONS AND CONTINUA OF ASSESSMENT

Assessment in Creative Disciplines: Designing an Assessment Schema Across the Span of the Degree Program

Category of Faculty Expectations and Observations	Information obtained prior to matriculation	Basic facts from institutional records	Information on student learning during the program of study				Information on outcomes at completion	Information on long-range outcomes
			Year 1	Year 2	Year	Year 4		
Acquisition of knowledge skills and abilities in the discipline	Portfolio or performance audition; Previous mentoring and/or studio relationships; Experience with ensembles, summer institutes, or other pre-professional experiences in high school or previous collegiate experience	Proxies: GPA; Academic Standing; Percentage of entering cohort of students retained in years 1, 2, 3, and 4; by gender, race, age; Progression of students through their program of study, by gender, race, age; Percentage of total entering cohort graduating; by gender, race, age; Years to degree.	Skill assessments in foundations courses; End of term juries or performances; Views of current students from surveys, student advisory groups; Views of faculty and advisors.	Skill assessments in foundations courses; End of term juries or performances; Views of current students from surveys, student advisory groups; Views of faculty and advisors.	Studio Critiques; End of term juries or performances; Views of current students from surveys, student advisory groups; Views of faculty and advisors; Active participation in student chapters of professional societies.	Studio Critiques; Senior Capstone project review by faculty and qualified external professionals; Success on licensure exams; Summarized information from evaluation by internship supervisors or other external evaluators; Views of current students from surveys, student advisory groups; Views of faculty and advisors.	Exit surveys and interviews; Panel of experts reads/reviews most recent capstone projects; Successful professional placement or admission to graduate study; Feedback from employers.	Alumni surveys such as SNAAP or interviews; Participation in professional societies within the discipline; review of career advancement from periodic review of vita.

Assessment in Creative Disciplines: Designing an Assessment Schema Across the Span of the Degree Program

Category of Faculty Expectations and Observations	Information obtained prior to matriculation	Basic facts from institutional records	Information on student learning during the program of study				Information on outcomes at completion	Information on long-range outcomes
			Year 1	Year 2	Year 3	Year 4		
Achievement of program-level student learning outcomes	Portfolio or performance audition; Academic preparation; SAT/MAT and advanced placement exams.	Proxies: Academic Standing; GPA; Percentage of entering cohort of students retained in years 1, 2, 3, and 4, by gender, race, age; Progression of students through their program of study, by gender, race, age; Percentage of total entering cohort graduating, by gender, race, age; Years to degree.	Assessment of general education competencies; Views of current students from surveys, student advisory groups; Views of faculty and advisors.	Assessment of general education competencies; Views of current students from surveys, student advisory groups; Views of faculty and advisors.	Studio Critiques; End of term juries or performances; Summarized information from evaluation by internship supervisors or other external evaluators; Views of current students from surveys, student advisory groups; Views of faculty and advisors; Active participation in student chapters of professional societies.	Studio Critiques; Senior Capstone project review by faculty and qualified external professionals; Success on licensure exams; Summarized information from evaluation by internship supervisors or other external evaluators; Views of current students from surveys, student advisory groups; Views of faculty and advisors.	Exit surveys and interviews; Panel of experts reads/reviews most recent capstone projects; Successful professional placement or admission to graduate study; Feedback from employers.	Alumni surveys such as SNAAP or interviews; Participation in professional societies within the discipline; review of career advancement from periodic review of vita

DIMENSIONS AND CONTINUA OF ASSESSMENT

Assessment in Creative Disciplines: Designing an Assessment Schema Across the Span of the Degree Program

Category of Faculty Expectations and Observations	Information obtained prior to matriculation	Basic facts from institutional records	Information on student learning during the program of study				Information on outcomes at completion	Information on long-range outcomes
			Year 1	Year 2	Year 3	Year 4		
Growth in metacognitive skills and self-reflective abilities	Writing samples; Interviews; Presentations; Experience with ensembles, summer institutes, or other pre-professional experiences in high school or previous collegiate experience	Proxies: GPA; Academic Standing; Percentage of entering cohort of students retained in years 1, 2, 3, and 4; by gender, race, age; Progression of students through their program of study, by gender, race, age; Percentage of total entering cohort graduating, by gender, race, age; Years to degree.	Assessments of reflective skills in foundations courses; End of term juries or performances; Views of current students from surveys, student advisory groups; views of faculty and advisors.	Assessments of reflective skills in foundations courses; End of term juries or performances; Views of current students from surveys, student advisory groups; views of faculty and advisors.	Studio Critiques; End of term juries or performances; Summarized information from evaluation by internship supervisors or other external evaluators; Views of current students from surveys, student advisory groups; Views of faculty and advisors; Active participation in student chapters of professional societies.	Senior Capstone project review by faculty and qualified external professionals; Studio Critiques; Success on licensure exams; Summarized information from evaluation by internship supervisors or other external evaluators; Views of current students from surveys, student advisory groups; views of faculty and advisors.	Exit surveys and interviews; Panel of experts reads/reviews most recent capstone projects; Successful professional placement or admission to graduate study; Feedback from employers.	Alumni surveys such as SNAAP or interviews; Participation in professional societies within the discipline; review of career advancement from periodic review of vita

Assessment in Creative Disciplines: Designing an Assessment Schema Across the Span of the Degree Program

Category of Faculty Expectations and Observations	Information obtained prior to matriculation — Basic facts from institutional records	Information on student learning during the program of study — Year 1	Year 2	Year 3	Year 4	Information on outcomes at completion	Information on long-range outcomes
Preparation for professional practice							
Experience with ensembles, summer institutes, or other pre-professional experiences in high school or previous collegiate experience	Proxies: GPA; Academic Standing; Percentage of cohort of entering students retained in years 1, 2, 3, and 4, by gender, race, age; Progression of students through their program of study, by gender, race, age; Percentage of total entering cohort graduating, by gender, race, age; Years to degree.	Skill assessments in foundations courses; End of term juries or performances; Views of current students from surveys, student advisory groups; views of faculty and advisors.	Skill assessments in foundations courses; End of term juries or performances; Views of current students from surveys, student advisory groups; views of faculty and advisors.	Studio Critiques; End of term juries or performances; Summarized information from evaluation by internship supervisors or other external evaluator and working professionals; Views of current students from surveys, student advisory groups; Active participation in student chapters of professional societies.	Studio Critiques; Senior Capstone project review by faculty and qualified external professionals; Success on licensure exams; Summarized information from evaluation by internship supervisors or other external evaluators; Views of current students from surveys, student advisory groups; views of faculty and advisors.	Exit surveys and interviews; Panel of experts reads/reviews most recent capstone projects; Successful professional placement or admission to graduate study; Feedback from employers.	Alumni surveys such as SNAAP or interviews; Participation in professional societies within the discipline; review of career advancement from periodic review of vita.

Considerations of Subjectivity and Objectivity in Assessment

As a final topic for this chapter, the difference between subjective and objective assessment constitutes yet another distinction that has been a frequent cause of miscommunication in assessment and merits some discussion, especially in the context of creative disciplines where informed judgment is so vital to the process of developing the creative artist or professional. The purpose of objective assessment is to remove bias and subjectivity by using an instrument -- usually a true-false or multiple-choice test, and frequently a standardized test -- that is valid, reliable, and fair. An objective assessment is one that needs no professional judgment to score it correctly, even though professional judgment may be required for appropriate interpretation.

Subjective assessments are those in which multiple ratings of varying quality are possible and which require professional expertise, awareness of quality in student or professional work, and the ability to render appropriate judgment to be appropriately scored. Such expertise is generally thought to be a prerequisite for assessing with validity, a notion developed at length by Eisner (1976) in his connoisseurship model of evaluation (see chapter on assessment models). In the case of subjective assessments, it is the ability of the expert rater to provide suitably granular assessment information, in many cases bound up with the context of a particular work or performance and not transferrable to other contexts, that provides suitable feedback and information for improvement.

High-level professional judgment is inextricably bound up with the process of mentoring and developing artists, designers, and other creative professionals. Since assessment in creative disciplines must generally be context-sensitive to be considered valid, one of the main challenges is to ensure that our subjective expert assessments are more reliable – that is, they will tend to produce similar results over time and situations. A great many of the assessments conducted in creative disciplines will be direct assessments of student work or performances, so it makes sense that we use well-developed rubrics to increase our ability to render not only context-sensitive ratings, but also ones about which colleagues can generally agree, and that would tend to be similar across time and administrations. Rubrics, a cornerstone of assessment practice in creative disciplines, are addressed at greater length in the chapter on technical foundations of assessment.

Summary

The foregoing chapter introduced the most appropriate purpose of assessment as a practice generally undertaken for ongoing (formative) improvement of teaching and learning as distinct from the judgment and accountability orientation of evaluation. The scope and locus of assessment was explained in terms of differing foci and assessment methods at the individual, course, program, and institutional levels. The notion of curriculum mapping was introduced to facilitate a holistic view across a program of study of how and where content relevant to particular student learning outcomes is introduced, reinforced, or mastered. The timing and placement of assessments across an entire program of study or student life cycle was dealt with at length, including a guide to assessments that may be appropriate to the four important student learning outcomes given. The chapter concluded with a discussion of subjectivity and objectivity in assessment and an exposition for the rationale behind developing and utilizing rubrics for much of the assessment work within creative disciplines.

References

Duke University, Academic Resource Center (n.d.). What is the difference between assessment and evaluation? Retrieved from http://duke.edu/arc/documents/The%20difference%20between%20assessment%20and%20evaluation.pdf.

Eisner, E. (1976). Educational Connoisseurship and Criticism: Their Form and Functions in Educational Evaluation. *Journal of Aesthetic Evaluation*, 10 (3-4): 135-150.

Ewell, P. (1984). *The self-regarding institution: information for excellence.* Boulder, CO: National Center for Higher Education Management Systems.

National Academy for Academic Leadership (n.d.), *Source:* http://www.thenationalacademy.org/readings/assessandeval.html.

Scriven, Michael (1967). "The methodology of evaluation". In Stake, R. E. *Curriculum evaluation.* Chicago: Rand McNally. American Educational Research Association (monograph series on evaluation, no. 1).

University of the Pacific (n.d.). Curriculum Map for B.A. in Jazz Studies. Used by permission.

Chapter 5: Models of Assessment in the Arts

One must not always think that feeling is everything. Art is nothing without form.
— Gustave Flaubert

The context of this chapter is to clarify those formal and informal models used for assessment in higher education, and to relate those models to assessment practice in design, performing, and representational arts. Of necessity, this chapter also touches on concepts of curriculum, learning design, and learning theory as they relate to formal organization of learning experiences. The focus of the chapter is at the department or program level, but includes tools that may be of interest to individual faculty members as they conceptualize and design course-level assessment. While there are multiple steps involved in creating a viable assessment model, the process tends to be much more iterative than linear since faculty thinking on assessment is bound to evolve, and changes in the planning environment are bound to have an effect as well. Larger concepts of institutional-level assessment, general education assessment, and systematic approaches to institutional effectiveness are not within scope of this chapter. We address specific assessment methods in a later chapter.

Beginning with the End in Mind

As a point of departure, the basic assumption of this chapter is that effective assessment depends upon thoughtful, purposive and cohesive educational design in which an individual student's artistic growth is accommodated, but in which details of educational design are not left to chance. Beginning with the end in mind, the standpoint of assessment is that effective program planning also depends on the development of intended learning outcomes for students, consisting of those discrete yet interrelated areas of knowledge, skills, abilities, and dispositions that together form a holistic representation of the professionally prepared artist. At its most basic, educational program planning also entails the articulation by faculty of those content areas necessary for mastery within the discipline, such as Itten's (1923) description of the Bauhaus basic course of instruction (see Figure 5.1).

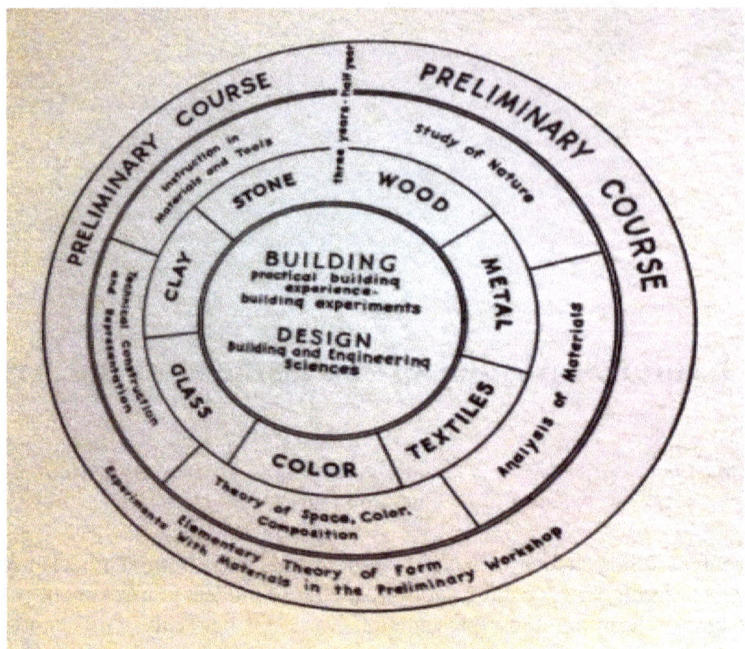

Figure 5.1: Bauhaus Basic Course of Instruction (Itten, 1923)

Beyond the articulation of intended student learning outcomes, and a description of content areas as the building blocks of learning design as in Itten's (1923) curriculum model, effective program planning further necessitates the creation of learning experiences that facilitate student acquisition of intended learning outcomes, and methods to ascertain the extent to which students have acquired and can demonstrate the intended learning outcomes at what faculty collectively determine to be the requisite level of proficiency. The use of a conceptual framework or model can substantially aid the construction of an assessment program driven by those learning outcomes. Volkwein (1998) describes numerous benefits of adopting a model-based perspective for assessment, noting that it encourages a clear overall purpose; provides a clear road map for posing assessment-related research questions, designing assessments, collecting data, testing hypotheses, and conducting analysis; causes us to develop a logical program flow or logic chart to help ascertain causality; and helps us focus our attention on the most important tasks, thus conserving both time and energy.

An enduring problem connected with the development and use of assessment models in art and design relates both to norms of career preparation and progression for faculty as well as to our individual training as creative artists and designers within our disciplines. We are trained as individual artists, hired as individual faculty by our institutions, and given discrete workload assignments. Too seldom are we specifically asked in our professional preparation to consider or articulate how, at what pace, and in what temporal sequence the optimal preparation of creative professionals should take place. Thus, we come to university teaching practice in many cases with an individual "solo artist" orientation to professional training and with very specific course assignments. In the absence of adequate exposure to pedagogical methods, as performers, designers, and artists we tend to fall back in our teaching on those mental models we acquired through our own training and experience, and expect what we learned long ago to work in our current pedagogical and studio practice. Yet excellence in any artistic endeavor demands ceaseless self-observation, reflection, critique, and improvement – something our students merit from our teaching practice as well, to ensure they are at the forefront as the creative forces of tomorrow.

A concept from the program evaluation literature may help clarify this point. In program evaluation, the concept of a logic model or program theory is used to explain how the developers of a social intervention or program expect it to work and result in desired outcomes (Chen, 2005). Frequently, the program theory is built on a set of unexamined assumptions that guide the program construction (Van Belle et al., 2010). Chen (2005) is widely credited as the founder of the influential theory-driven approach to program evaluation, one in which the implicit assumptions of why a program should work are surfaced through observation and reflection, operationally defined, put to the test, and collaboratively refined as appropriate. Similarly, good assessment demands of us as creative practitioners that we uncover the untested assumptions in our pedagogy, reflect upon our practice, assess the extent to which our students are attaining the desired outcomes, and make adjustments as appropriate.

Furthermore, while our personal creative and scholarly work is appropriately within our individual purview, it is important to consider that the design of an educational program of study belongs to no one faculty member individually, but is rather the common intellectual property of the faculty as a whole (Wergin, 2003). Assessment design thus merits a collective and deep consideration by faculty within a department or program of curriculum purposes, content, goals for student learning, and information on student competency that can be shared and used to further refine the design of the program.

Theories of Learning

As part of the conceptual toolkit for putting together appropriate assessment models, contemporary higher education assessment practice has come to include a consideration of learning theories as a basis for departure. Theories of learning can assist faculty in thinking through the assumptions they hold concerning the conditions under which students learn, and in moving from a passive theory in use (Chen, 2005) to an educational model built on our best understanding of the learning process. An understanding of learning theories can also aid our understanding of how to facilitate learning in a manner that accommodates individual students – a key aspect in artistic formation within any creative discipline.

While the scope of this chapter precludes anything more than a brief mention of major types of learning theories, their consideration as part of the framework for a well-designed assessment model is crucial. Fortunately, numerous summaries of learning theories are available. Excellent examples include those by Dunn (2002) and Lepi (2012). Briefly, learning theories may be grouped under four major headings: behaviorism, cognitivism, constructivism, and connectivism. Behaviorism concentrates on observable behavior and how that may be altered through instructional stimuli. B.F. Skinner (1968; 1961, with James Holland) is preeminent representative of this school of thought. Cognitivism, represented by authors such as Piaget (1975/1936) and Gagne (1985) deals with how knowledge may be gained, stored, and retrieved through encoding and reworking of cognitive structures, for example through feedback to students. Under constructivism, represented by writers such as Dewey (1938, 1966) and Vygotsky (1962), knowledge is seen as socially constructed. Learners engage in the process of knowledge construction through interaction and collaboration with others. Finally, connectivism speaks to the basis of knowledge as being increasingly external to the learner, distributed within personal and technological networks, changing rapidly, and fundamentally chaotic in nature. From a connectivist standpoint, much learning consists in knowing how to make connections among information sources and how best to leverage those sources within a rapidly evolving knowledge environment. Notable authors include Siemens (2004) and Downes (2007). Learning theories are highly relevant in that a well-designed assessment model might take into account insights from behaviorism, cognitivism, and constructivism, and with the inclusion of insights from connectivism, yielding an appropriate blend of learning theory as a scaffold for learning design and models of assessment within creative disciplines.

Perspectives or Conceptual Lenses for Assessment

With student learning outcomes and an appropriate theory-informed perspective developed, the next step is to consider what may be the most appropriate perspective(s) through which we choose to view assessment of student learning. The process may be viewed through numerous conceptual lenses, depending on our perspective and our intent. Suskie (2004) for instance, describes a variety of perspectives on assessment. These include:

- Normative or peer comparisons;
- Comparisons to an internal or external standard such as benchmarks, best in class perspectives, standards of professional associations, student capability/potential vs. achievement; and meeting specific department or college achievement goals;
- Comparisons involving change over time, such as value-added, pre-post test, and historical trends or improvement over time;
- Holistic comparisons, including assessment of student strengths, needs for improvement, opportunities for enhanced teaching and learning, and threats to student achievement; and
- Economic comparisons, such as return on investment, opportunity costs of one method over another, and the balance between efficiency and effectiveness.

By making a collective effort to think through and discuss the desired or most useful perspectives for a program or department's assessment design, faculty can more effectively design the system to yield results that will be useful for educational and programmatic decisions.

Models/Frameworks of Assessment in Art and Design

A variety of models or conceptual frameworks for assessment have been proposed in higher education overall. Within creative disciplines, an emerging body of assessment models also exists. These models vary in their consideration of learning theory and learning design, their attention to structure, and their overall specificity. The following discussion is intended to provide a sample of available approaches rather than an exhaustive compendium, to offer a cornucopia of possibilities for faculty to consider as a basic scaffold for their assessment efforts, and to note how each of these models might be applied in practice. To facilitate the discussion, assessment models are described here as belonging to several broad categories: general higher education assessment models; theory-driven approaches to assessment in creative disciplines; and finally, structural models for assessment design in creative disciplines.

General Assessment Models in Higher Education

General higher education assessment models are those that have been applied across a number of situations, institutions, and curricula in higher education but that are not avowedly designed to accommodate the nuances of creative disciplines. Among such models, Alexander Astin's theory of student involvement and Input-Environment-Output (I-E-O) model stand out as preeminent.

Alexander Astin: Theory of Student Involvement and I-E-O Model

Astin's (1984/1999) description of a theory of student involvement and his (1991) articulation of the I-E-O model have provided a widely-used conceptual foundation for educational research and assessment programs across the country. The central theorem of Astin's theory of student involvement is deceptive in its simplicity: "[T]he theory of student involvement argues that a particular curriculum, to achieve the effects intended, must elicit sufficient student effort and investment of energy to bring about the desired learning and development" (1984/1999, p. 522). Astin's (1991) I-E-O model provides a conceptual model on which to frame the theory of student involvement. In the I-E-O model, inputs consist of pre-college characteristics, such as the student's prior experiences, demographic makeup, and background. The second element of the model, the student's environment, consists of those experiences, programs, processes, staff, faculty and other students, and culture encountered during college. Finally, the category of outcomes includes the knowledge, skills, abilities, dispositions, beliefs, and behaviors following college. In addition to understanding each of these elements separately, we gain a much fuller understanding by looking at the interactions among the elements of the I-E-O model – for example by controlling for variances in student capabilities at the beginning of a program when we are looking at overall gains in student learning over the course of that program. A graphic depiction of this model appears below as Figure 5.2.

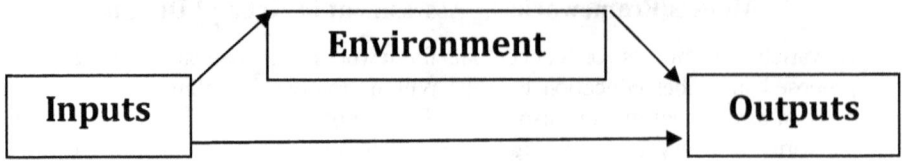

Figure 5.2. I-E-O model
Source: Astin (1991)

In addition to the three basic elements in the I-E-O model, Astin offers five postulates or assumptions: First, involvement requires investing energy in tasks, people, and activities, from the overall student experience to specific projects such as a design or performance. Second, involvement varies by subject or area in a single student's experience at different times as well as varying among students. Third, both qualitative and quantitative aspects are involved. Hours of study can be measured quantitatively, but application to a task within those hours of study may need to be assessed by other means. Fourth, and perhaps most importantly, the extent of learning and student development associated with a program of study will have a direct relationship to the amount and quality of student academic and psychosocial involvement in that program: more involvement will lead to more learning. Finally, the extent to which a program, policy, or practice is effective will be directly related to how well it is able to increase student involvement. (Astin, 1984/1999, p. 519).

How useful might such a general theory be applicable as an assessment model within creative disciplines? Astin (1984/1999) sees his theory as a major step forward from thinking about the collegiate and academic experience as essentially an impenetrable black box, and nearly three decades after its introduction, student involvement theory and the I-E-O model still have relevance. Consideration of input factors such as an applicant's portfolio, audition, or high school achievement, in addition to guiding the acceptance and initial placement of a student, can give us a baseline for understanding the student's development and gains through a program of study. Understanding how students take advantage or fail to take advantage of student chapters of professional associations, gallery openings, performances, social activities, and involvement in their studies may help us understand how and why they thrive or fail to thrive in creative disciplines. Assessment of student learning outcomes and career outcomes following graduation will help us understand the extent to which our overall curriculum is achieving its desired aims, and how relevant it is to current creative practice. Finally, Astin (1984/1999) reminds us that as instructors we should focus more on what our students are actually doing, how involved they are, and how much energy they are devoting to their creative discipline – and less on our specific content or teaching technique. As he notes, "Teaching is a complex art. And, like other art forms, it may suffer if the artist focuses exclusively on technique. Instructors can be more effective if they focus on the intended outcomes of their pedagogical efforts: achieving maximum student involvement and learning" (1984/1999, p.526).

Theory-driven Assessment Models in Creative Disciplines

In general, theory-driven assessment models are those that exhibit a strong theoretical basis, but not necessarily a detailed model of practice through which to realize the model. We provide two examples of models within the theory-driven genre.

Leslie Cunliffe: The Metacognitive Approach

Within the context of art education, Leslie Cunliffe has long researched the connection among self-reflective artistic activities, growth in metacognition in students and pedagogical practices that promote such growth. A strong proponent of increasingly self-regulated learning in creative disciplines, Cunliffe (2007, 2008a, 2012) describes the philosophic basis and outlines of an assessment model, one grounded in deliberately developed procedural and situational knowledge and dispositions and brought to fruition through teaching practices that promote the growth of metacognitive abilities and ethical self-knowledge in students necessary for them to flourish as creative professionals.

Cunliffe (2007) outlines a complex taxonomy of those cognitive processes, traits, dispositions, and characteristics necessary to develop the capacity for self-regulation in creative performance that truly reflects higher-order thinking. In the taxonomy, he identifies a set of six broad categories within which those strategies, dispositions, characteristics and traits may be identified, including

- Common strategies needed for self-regulated learning, such as reduction of a task or problem into its components;
- Cognitive strategies needed for self-regulated learning, such as generating alternative solutions;
- Dispositions needed to be cultivated for self-regulated learning, such as being strategic and planning a course of action;
- Cognitive aspects that need to be cultivated for self-regulated creativity, such as convergent thinking abilities;
- Character traits needed to be cultivated for self-regulated creativity, such as being curious and being able to tolerate ambiguity; and
- Character traits that teachers have to foster to support the development of self-regulated creativity, such as promoting self-evaluation in students (2007, p. 8).

While a detailed discussion of the taxonomy is beyond the scope of this chapter, two points are worth stressing. First is Cunliffe's (2007) insistence that the strategies, dispositions, characteristics, and traits in the taxonomy must be used and practiced interactively with one another for successful integration of the model. Second, it bears pointing out that the taxonomy may be used as a basis for developing intended learning outcomes for a program of study whose overarching purpose is the development of self-reflective and metacognitively aware creative professionals. As to how faculty may actually organize a program of study to maximize student metacognitive development, Cunliffe (2007) provides only high-level guidance, indicating that instructors will have the task of translating the numerous variables across all six categories of the taxonomy into appropriate pedagogies to catalyze truly self-regulated, strategic forms of creativity and learning in students.

Given the emphasis in his model on self-reflection and the ability to self-regulate through heightened metacognitive abilities, Cunliffe posits that the notion of a model for assessment must shift from an instructor-focused standpoint to one where students must bear much of the responsibility for self-assessment:

> In this respect, assessment for learning how to learn to cultivate strategic intelligence relocates normative properties away from the teacher making judgments about temporary acts or mindsets, in favour of supporting the cultivation of stable dispositions, character traits and cognitive processes that enable students' to accurately form judgements about their own learning, which in turn might lead to genuine flourishing based on the content that makes up the cognitive unconscious (2007, p. 10).

If the locus of assessment is to be radically shifted to the student, with the faculty providing guidance for the student to engage in strategies that will lead to higher self-regulation as an artist, the assessment model itself begins to look more like a series of feedback and feed-forward mechanisms, based upon established criteria for success – using the taxonomy as a basis. In Figure 5.3 below, Cunliffe (2012) depicts such an assessment model as a scaffold whereby a basic plan is established; periodic formative assessments take place that enable the student to look ahead and feed forward areas for further development, while nevertheless conscious of the instructor's feedback.

Time →

Assessment Plan:	Formal formative self-assessment 1:	Formal formative self-assessment 2:	Summative self-assessment:
➤ Establish and share criteria for success	❏ Feed forward	❏ Feed forward	❏ Feedback evaluation
➤ Describe learning targets	➤ Audit the learning	➤ Audit the learning	➤ Audit the learning

- Establish and share the role of different forms of assessment:
  - Formal formative assessment 1
  - Formal formative assessment 2
  - Summative assessment
  - Ongoing ipsative monitoring

- Feed forward to next module

Figure 5.3: An Example of Using Assessment for Learning
Source: *Adapted from Cunliffe (2012)*

Given the strength of the philosophic underpinnings of Cunliffe's approach and his insistence of the primacy of student growth in metacognition as vital to the development of the creative professional, the fundamental insights proceeding from this model simply cannot be ignored in any fully-developed assessment schema. As he notes, "The one function of assessment that has arguably been least catered for is its role in enabling students to learn how to regulate their own learning and creativity" (2007, p.2).

Elliott Eisner—Connoisseurship Model

In contrast to more quantitative models of assessment, the work of Elliott Eisner (1976, 1985) stands out. Eisner (1976) originally developed a connoisseurship model that is predicated on subject, perceptual, and background expertise of the evaluator ("connoisseurship") and the evaluator's ability to offer cogent observations at a granular level ("criticism") that serves as a basis for bringing about improvement – not just accountability. The model was developed in reaction to what Eisner perceived to be a reductionist tendency in evaluation – the view that educational achievement that cannot be counted or directly described through language must therefore not exist. Eisner notes that the arts in particular have internally referential languages that exist outside of written language and must be approached through metaphor and non-numeric description.

Criticism, in Eisner's (1976) model, operates at multiple levels: descriptive, interpretive, and evaluative, including the identification of dominant themes or qualities ("thematics") in the phenomena being examined. These differing levels on which criticism operates all create the possibility for lack of agreement among evaluators. Two reviewers may not agree on the description of a performance, for example, let alone their interpretations or their ascriptions of quality to the performance. To ensure that standards of credibility in evaluation are met, the connoisseurship model rests on several pillars of qualitative research. First, criticism must be corroborated through triangulation and support from multiple data sources ("Structural corroboration"). The fit between critical observations and the actual student artifacts, conditions, or facts at hand must be validated. Second, it must meet the test of agreement by multiple competent raters ("consensual validation"). Finally, it must be sufficiently detailed and multi-faceted to re-educate and deepen our perceptions, and bring to light those aspects of the phenomena being evaluated that might not otherwise have been surfaced. From this standpoint, the role of the evaluator in the connoisseurship model is to bring out aspects of a work or performance that non-experts might overlook or fail to perceive.

Given its flexibility and its reliance on triangulated, validated forms of expert panel review, Eisner's perspective has been widely used as an evaluation framework in creative disciplines. A common application of Eisner's model is in academic program review, as noted by Conrad and Wilson (1985), where external reviewers are engaged to conduct a holistic expert-based evaluation of an academic program.

Structural Models for Assessment Design in Creative Disciplines

Assessing Creativity: Strategies and Tools To Support Teaching and Learning in Architecture and Design (Williams and Askland, 2012)

In *Assessing Creativity: Strategies and Tools To Support Teaching and Learning in Architecture and Design,* Williams and Askland (2012) offer what is certainly one of more comprehensive assessment models for creative disciplines. While developed as a general assessment model for creativity in design and architecture in the context of Australian institutions, the model may be readily adapted to use in other creative disciplines, college and university systems, and geographic locations.

As a basis upon which to ground the model, Williams and Askland (2012) develop a conceptual framework for thinking about creativity, consisting of four Ps—person, process, product, and press (environmental factors/context). According to their definition of creativity, students (persons) go through a recognizable set of steps (process) to develop a creative work (product), while doing so within a particular situation or context that involves recognizable environmental factors (press). The model, referred to as an assessment process map, is depicted in **Figure 5.4** below.

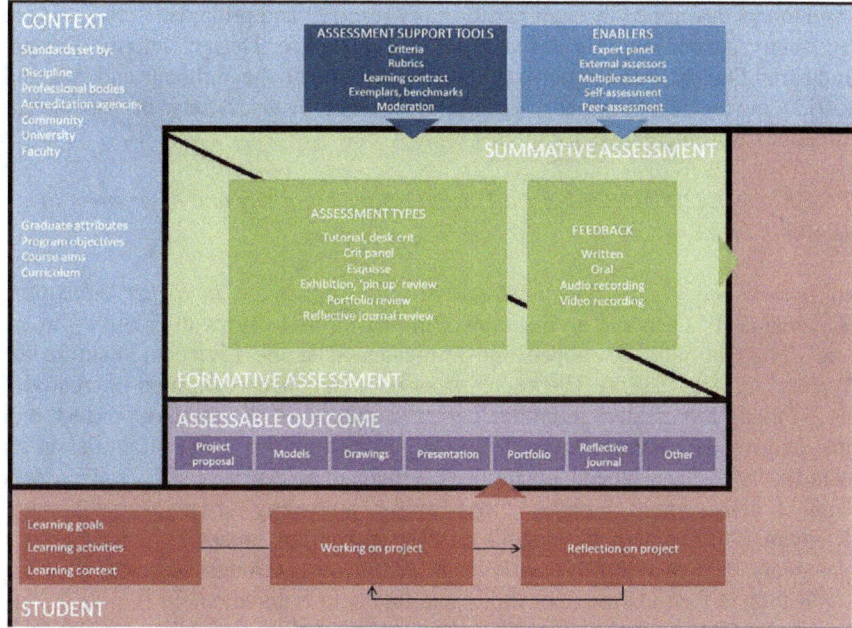

Figure 5.4: Map of Assessment Process.
Source: Williams and Askland (2012).

In discussing how their model might be applied to assessment within specific disciplines and situations, Williams and Askland (2012) note that a careful consideration should be given to how the elements of the model will be applied and to what purpose – formative (improvement-oriented) or summative (judgment-oriented) assessment. First, the context or environment should be considered. Second, the actual medium of expression – the way the students can demonstrate their acquisition of the desired learning outcomes - should be taken into consideration. Third, the choice of assessment method needs to be linked to the actual learning outcomes being assessed. Finally, the assessment method must correlate to appropriate assessment support tools (such as rubrics or exemplars) and enablers (such as expert panels or peer assessors). With these considerations in mind, the authors offer four key framing questions to assist in the design of a specific assessment regime:

1. What is the overriding goal for learning, underpinning the assessment task, and how may the task assist the students as future practitioners?
2. What is the best medium for the students to enhance their learning and explore and develop the skills targeted by the task?
3. How can the outcome of the task be assessed; what is the most appropriate assessment type?
4. What assessment support tool and/or enabler may be used for the assessment task to ensure that the assessment is equal, reliable, accountable, valid, repeatable, and sustainable? (Williams and Askland, 2012, p.24)

As a model developed through participatory research and grounded in the practice of faculty across multiple design fields (Architecture, Design, Interior Design, Industrial Design, Landscape Architecture, and Other), the Williams and Askland (2012) model is robust and generalizable to a wide variety of assessment situations within creative disciplines.

Paul Kleiman (2005), Beyond the Tingle Factor: Creativity and Assessment in Higher Education

In *Beyond the Tingle Factor: creativity and assessment in higher education*, Kleiman (2005) sets out an assessment model for assessment of creativity in art and design initially developed and implemented at the Liverpool Institute for Performing Arts (LIPA). The system is based on a conceptualization of creativity as involving the creative individual, creative processes, the creative product, and the creative environment/context in complex interactions – not dissimilar in its complexity to the conceptualization of Williams and Askland (2012). To assess student achievement within a measurable, ascending order of complexity, Kleiman (2005) adopted Fennel's (1993) lexicon of creativity – basically, a taxonomy that recognizes creativity as progressing through four stages: from replication to formulation, innovation and finally to origination.

The LIPA assessment model was constructed specifically to provide a reliable, valid, and fair assessment of creative work using six standard practices and emphases, thus providing for comparability across students:

- **Presentation/Production** i.e. the finished product presented to an audience
- **Process** i.e. the journey that led to the product
- **Idea** i.e. the ideas that informed both the process and the product.
- **Technical** i.e. the quality and utility of the technical features of the product and the skills with which they were assembled and/or operated
- **Documentation** i.e. research, design, planning, evaluation etc.
- **Interview** i.e. the student's ability to articulate their understanding, utili[z]ation and application and use of any of the above. (Kleiman, 2005, p.16)

The system at LIPA was based on several notions. First, students in creative disciplines would be working at differing levels and in different ways, producing a variety of works through both differing processes and methods. This flexibility had to be accounted for in the system. Second, to function properly, assessment had to be embedded into teaching and learning rather than being an add-on, and had to be perceived as integral to the learning processes. Third, the conventions and practice of assessment within each discipline had to be appropriate for that discipline, such that students were actively engaged in the assessment process rather than being passive objects of assessment. Supported by these basic precepts, the assessment system was particularized to each discipline, and faculty developed both grading ranges and detailed criteria for assessment within each grading range. Taking particular care to build an assessment system that would not be dismissed as reductionist, would retain flexibility in its design, and would allow for individual variation, Kleiman and his colleagues at LIPA developed a system of "negotiated assessment" (2005, p. 15) with the support of their chief external examiner, Sir Ken Robinson. Within this system, students could negotiate the relative weightings of each field or dimension being assessed in the context of an assessment interview with their major professors. For example, a student who wanted to take a substantial creative risk in their work could negotiate to have greater assessment weighting placed on their creative ideas, processes and documentation and relatively less weigh on presentation or production.

External accountability was built in from the outset in that the LIPA assessment model was also developed to meet quality and standards frameworks in the UK and the requirements for cross-institutional validation within that system. As a central feature of this assessment model, a presentation or production of a final performance or product was required, and each individual student was required to undertake a periodic assessment interview with an expert panel of assessors of 30-40 minutes duration to demonstrate their learning and artistic accomplishment. Assessment interviews were conducted by a panel of faculty, who would use the assessment criteria to form questions for the student. Questions were posed on an ascending level of complexity. The point at which negative responses to the questions outweighed positive responses signified to the faculty review panel and the student that the assessment of the student's work had reached its highest level.

The advantages of such a structured yet simultaneously flexible model for assessment in creative disciplines should be apparent. As an overall college assessment schema, it can be implemented in a contextually appropriate manner within each discipline and embedded in programs of study for both formative and summative assessment. The use of set assessment criteria and an expert panel enhances the possibility of conducting valid and reliable assessment of student work. The inclusion of flexibility and negotiating the weighting of the assessment criteria ensures that students had a voice in the process and were more likely to perceive it as a fair assessment as well as an environment in which they could take artistic risks to achieve substantial artistic growth.

Summary

This chapter has dealt with formal and informal models used for assessment in higher education. In each case, the models presented have been related to assessment practice in creative disciplines. As a basis for understanding assessment models, the chapter touched on major theories of learning, perspectives on assessment and evaluation. In the context of this chapter we discussed generalized assessment models, represented by Alexander Astin's (1984/1999; 1991) work. Next, we explored theory-driven models, where the underlying theory is specified but the practical details of developing an assessment schema are left to the practitioner. Cunliffe's (2007, 2008a, 2012) metacognitive approach was presented along with Eisner's (1976) Connoisseurship Model. Finally, we provided substantial detail on two structural models for assessment in creative disciplines. From Australia, Williams and Askland's (2012) comprehensive assessment model provided us with in-depth insight into a workable assessment design that resulted from a multi-institution study. From the United Kingdom, Paul Kleiman's (2005) assessment model, originally developed at the Liverpool Institute for Performing Arts, provided yet another view of a well-developed and highly applicable model for assessment in creative disciplines.

Our intent in this chapter has been to provide a representative sample of the assessment frameworks and models that may be utilized by faculty, departments, and colleges in framing the design and operation of assessment systems. Further chapters will explore assessment instrumentation, tools, methods of analysis, and ways of bringing faculty together to review results and implement programmatic adjustments based on their findings.

References

Astin, A. (1984/1999) Student involvement: A developmental theory for higher education. *Journal of College Student Development*, Sept. – Oct. 1999. 40 (5): 518-529.

Astin, A. (1991). *Assessment for excellence: The philosophy and practice of assessment and evaluation in higher education*. New York: Greenwood Publishing Company.

Bruner, J.S. (1966). *Toward a theory of instruction*. Cambridge, MA: Belkapp Press.

Chen, H.T., 2005, *Practical program evaluation. Assessing and improving planning, implementation and effectiveness*, Sage Publications, Thousand Oaks, California.

Conrad, C. and Wilson, R. (1985). Academic Program Reviews: Institutional Expectations and Controversies. ASHE-ERIC Higher Education Report No. 5. Washington, D.C.: Association for the Study of Higher Education.

Cunliffe, L. (2007). Using Assessment in Knowledge-Rich Forms of Learning and Creativity to Nurture Self-Regulated Strategic Intelligence. Paper presented at Creativity or Conformity? Building Cultures of Creativity in Higher Education, University of Wales Institute and Higher Education Academy, Cardiff, Wales, January 8-10, 2007.

Cunliffe, L. (2008a). Using Assessment to Nurture Knowledge-Rich Creativity. *Innovations in Education and Teaching International, 45 (3): 309-317.*

Cunliffe, L. (2012). Art education 'as if' for future flourishing. In Addison, N. and Burgess, L. (Eds.), *Debates in Art and Design Education*, New York: Routledge, p. 192-193.

Dewey, John. (1938). *Experience and Education*. New York: Macmillan.

Dewey, John. (1966). *Democracy and Education*. New York: Free Press.

Dunn, L. (2002). *Theories of Learning*. Oxford: Oxford Brookes University Centre for Staff and Learning Development. Retrieved January 2, 2013 from http://www.brookes.ac.uk/services/ocsld/resources/briefing_papers/learning_theories.pdf .

Downes, S. (2005). An Introduction to Connective Knowledge. in Hug, Theo (ed.) (2007): Media, Knowledge & Education - Exploring new Spaces, Relations and Dynamics in Digital Media Ecologies. Proceedings of the International Conference held on June 25-26, 2007. November 27, 2007.

Eisner, E. (1976). Educational Connoisseurship and Criticism: Their Form and Functions in Educational Evaluation. *Journal of Aesthetic Evaluation*, 10 (3-4): 135-150.

Eisner, Elliot W. (1985). *The art of educational evaluation: a personal view*. London: Falmer Press.

Fennel, E. (1993) Categorising Creativity. *Competence and Assessment* 23:7. Referenced in Kleiman, P. (2005). Beyond the Tingle Factor: creativity and assessment in higher education. Paper presented at the Economic and Social Research Council (ESRC) seminar, University of Strathclyde, Scotland. November 2005.

Gagne, R. (1985). *The Conditions of Learning* (4th ed). New York: Holt, Rinehart & Winston.

Holland, J. and Skinner, B., (1961), *The Analysis of Behavior: A Program for Self Instruction*. New York: McGraw Hill.

Itten, Johannes (1923, reprint 1964). Design and Form: The Basic Course at the Bauhaus and Later. New York: Reinhold Publishing Company.

Kleiman, P. (2005). Beyond the Tingle Factor: creativity and assessment in higher education. Paper presented at the Economic and Social Research Council (ESRC) seminar, University of Strathclyde, Scotland. November 2005.

Lepi, Katie (2012). A Simple Guide to 4 Complex Learning Theories. *Edudemic*, Monday, December 24, 2012. Retrieved from http://edudemic.com/2012/12/a-simple-guide-to-4-complex-learning-theories on January 2, 2013.

Piaget, J (1975/1936). *La naissance de l'intelligence chez l'enfant. [Emergence of intelligence in the child] in Three theories of cognitive representation and their evaluation standards of training effect*. Neuchatel: Delachaux et Nieslé/Heerlson, The Netherlands: Heerlson.

Siemens, G. (2004, updated 2005). *Connectivism: A Learning Theory for the Digital Age*. Retrieved January 2, 2013 from http://www.elearnspace.org/Articles/connectivism.htm .

Skinner, B., *The Technology of Teaching*, 1968. New York: Appleton-Century-Crofts.

Suskie, Linda. (2004). *Assessing Student Learning: A Common Sense Guide*. Bolton, MA: Anker Publishing.

Van Belle et al., (2010). How to develop a theory-driven evaluation design? Lessons learned from an adolescent sexual and reproductive health programme in West Africa. *BMC Public Health* 2010, 10:741 http://www.biomedcentral.com/1471-2458/10/741

Volkwein, J.F. (1998). Managing a Program of Outcomes Assessment, Workshop presented at the 37th Annual Forum of the Association for Institutional Research. Retrieved January 27, 2013 from http://www.rosehulman.edu/IRPA/IR/inair/workshop.html .

Vygotsky, D. (1962). *Thought and language*. Cambridge, MA: MIT Press.

Wergin, J. (2003). *Departments that Work*. Boston: Anker Publishing Company.
Williams, A. and Askland, H. (2012). *Assessing creativity: Strategies and tools to support teaching and learning in architecture and design*, Final Report 2012. Sydney, Australia: Australian Government Office for Learning and Teaching.

Chapter 6: Challenges to Assessing the Aesthetic

In the difficult are the friendly forces, the hands that work on us.
— Rainer Maria Rilke

The assessment movement has been in full swing for more than two decades now, and like any new initiative in higher education, assessment has presented its own set of challenges. Some of these challenges include suspicion as to the use of its results and if it would be a passing trend (similar to the glut and then rather fast demise of many first year experience classes at universities around the U.S. in the early 2000s), concern over the potential increase in workload for faculty and staff, and a question of the practicality of assessment (i.e. what to assess, when to assess, and how often, and then what to do with and how to present the results).

Few academic disciplines have had a more challenging time doing systematized assessment than those in the arts, even though evaluation has always been a part of the artistic process and master artist-student relationship. Or as Ross (1994) writes, "Assessing is something creators, performers, and arts viewers do all the time, an on-going means of charting growth, mastering new skills, and monitoring one's own achievement" (p. 13). The reasons for the challenges can seem myriad (many will be explored in this chapter), but can be divided into three main categories:

- challenges with colleagues
- challenges of structure and practicality
- challenges in logistics and consistency.

Johnson and Gould (2009) write, "Departments in the arts and humanities are often inhospitable environments for assessment of learning outcomes. For one thing, student learning outcomes in these disciplines is not easily quantified" (p. 33). Assessing the aesthetic also presents structural and practical challenges, some caused by the temporal nature of some art forms or because there is no universally accepted pedagogy or technical standards (or these may vary with genre), and others caused by the subjectivity that goes into all art evaluation. There are also the two questions if the act of choosing what to assess creates value or emphasis in the discipline, and how process and product can both be a part of arts assessment, especially in light of state departments of education and the National Assessment of Educational Progress Arts Education Assessment trying to create frameworks for artistic discipline assessments on the K-12 level.

Challenges with Colleagues

First, let us tackle the challenge of colleagues being assessment's worst enemy. Artist Marc Chagall said, "All colors are friends of their neighbors and the lovers of their opposites;" if only we could say the same about our colleagues in academia. Some faculty, staff, and administration, as well as some students, are resistant to and feel threatened by change. These people have been labeled "CAVEs", which stands for Colleagues Against Virtually Everything. You know who they are; you've worked beside them for years. And any time assessment is brought up, or the creation and exploration of student learning outcomes, or the mining of data for institutional effectiveness, these CAVEs spout reasons why these activities are not good ideas, albeit the objections could be in the guise of "too much extra work", "not enough time to do the work", "the data could interfere with the way or what we teach", "the infringement upon academic freedom," "the administration becoming too controlling," etc. Or as Johnson and Gould (2009) write, "...department chairs and faculty members, having survived the culture wars of the 1990s, are understandably wary of any initiative that seems to demand a justification of what they do" (p. 33). Long-time academics have seen trends come and go. They remember putting in many hours and much effort on past initiatives only to see them eventually fall out of favor or focus when new administrators have taken the helm, or when the public and politicians have shifted their priorities to other things.

But for assessment to work, for it to be meaningful, manageable, and sustainable, and for its results to be incorporated in future student learning, faculty have to take ownership of it because, after all, faculty own the curriculum, and because "When...departments take ownership of the process, assessment becomes a powerful tool in making an effective case for scarce resources" (Johnson & Gould, 2009, p.33).

This last point could also help when dealing with colleagues whose underlying objections may be rooted in fear. Sometimes it is difficult for faculty to separate out how student learning reflects on the faculty member personally and how it solely reflects the student's experience of learning, discovery, creation, perception, knowing, and integrating. Assessments are not a snapshot in time of one particular skill or piece of knowledge (that collection of information is the purview of tests and other one-of evaluation methods), but assessments are more deliberate collections of information used to provide student feedback (Raodcy, Boyle, 1987). The most effective assessments are integrated into the curriculum and are ongoing. They are not focused on the work of one particular course but on skills taught and built on throughout the entire curriculum. Students in the arts, just like in the sciences and other disciplines, need to learn accepted bodies of terms and concepts (that can be tested by quizzes and exams), but then these need to be internalized and Bloom's 1956 taxonomy, Anderson and colleagues' 2001 revision, along with Harlow's psychomotor learning structure

(1972), need to be converged into affective learning. And in the arts that results in an emotional commitment to the work itself (Johnson & Gould, 2009, p. 36).

One other objection that colleagues may have with assessment is that it takes the creativity out of arts. Boughton (2008) writes, "A popular and long held belief of many educators is that assessment is an antidote to creative behavior. Those who hold that view argue that students' creativity will be inhibited if they know their art making activities will be assessed because assessment will cause them to become anxious and afraid to take risks" (p. 2). From this standpoint, one could surmise that the study of 16th and 18th century counterpoint should somehow negatively affect one's ability to listen and be moved by music. We know quite the opposite to be true, that through understanding composition we become better listeners and achieve a more in-depth response to it. Part of the role of an arts educator: to balance the crafting of a safe space for creativity with appropriate rigor and a solid critique. Tonski (2010) writes that "creativity requires risk-taking," and that "this requires some perception of safety." He suggests asking students what motivates them since "being heard/validated garners buy-in and this is a building block for risk taking" (p.1). Boughton says that it is important to set up "interrelated curriculum and assessment strategies that promote rather than inhibit creative outcomes" (p. 7).

Challenges of Structure and Practicality

After setting up that safe space, then we must determine what to assess. Knowing what to assess when one performance or charrette or portfolio brings together so many variables and things that could be assessed is part of the challenge when assessing the aesthetic. As Robert Cohen (2013) so aptly summarizes in *Theatre*:

> When she goes onstage, the actor faces a great many levels of awareness. She must interact and she must perform. She must relate in some way to a text, a theatre, an audience, scenery pieces, costumes, props, the demands of her director, the behaviour of her fellow actors, and the actions of the stage crew. She must also deal with possible distractions: the awareness of potential critics that may be in the audience, of the state of her own career, and of the offstage relationships she maintains – or wishes to maintain – with her fellow performers. She must deal with the anxieties of stage fright, vocal tension, physical clumsiness, the terror of forgetting her lines, of drying up emotionally and – worst of all-of letting her confidence sag. She must be spontaneous without thinking about being spontaneous, and without overtly appearing to try to be spontaneous. She must work within a fixed script and yet make the words seem to emanate from her own mind and not from some-ago printed text. She must create the play's character and yet be sufficiently personal and idiosyncratic to seem humanly alive. She must fit into the play's style without losing her sense of humanity. She must be credible and, in the best sense of the word, theatrical.

So many nuances go into a student's culminating performance, project, paper, and/or portfolio that determining where to start the assessment and what exactly to assess can seem like an overwhelming task. And when what you need to assess is a live performance, or something equally temporal, how do you determine on what to focus, when even the very act of assessment itself can cause you to miss what you are assessing? "For the performing and creating portions of the assessment, the problem…is too live. One either needs numerous on-site scorers, or more feasibly, the capability of video-taping the students' efforts for later off-site scoring because it is so difficult to 'see' everything in a single viewing…" (Ross, 1994, p. 11).

But in videotaping, Ross (1994) and others argue that the interplay between performers is lost and becomes un-assessable, and this is interplay and loss of immediacy is part of the attributes of a live performance. There's also a question in group performances whether to focus on the contribution of an individual performance within the group or on the group (Eisner, 1993).

Part of the challenge of determining what to assess comes from art being highly subjective, and because no single measure exists that can truly capture a student's behaviors, knowledge, and experience. Ross (1994) writes:

> Despite the widespread practices of assessment in professional dance, rubrics here turn out to be vague and frameworks highly personal and idiosyncratic. Interviews with several leaders in the field of classical ballet competitions (the most standardized dance genre and the one with the most frequent competitions) reveal that while each adjudicator knows what first-, second-, and third-rate dancing looks like when it is happening, spelling out the precise attributes of each level independent of a contestant is all but impossible (p. 8).

A second problem with rubrics and evaluation is that sometimes the things that are looked at are sometimes attributes and not precise skills (Ross, 1994, p. 9). Webster's defines a skill as "1) the ability, coming from one's knowledge, practice, aptitude, etc., to do something well; 2) competent excellence in performance; expertness; dexterity;" whereas, an attribute is "an inherent characteristic; an accidental quality" (*Merriam-Webster's Collegiate Dictionary*, 1999, p. 75). One is teachable and can be improved upon; the other, according to the definition, cannot be taught.

Another challenge to assessment practices goes hand-in-hand with determining what exactly to assess. Once one determines what to assess and how to assess it, this choice influences what students believe to be important (Smith, 2013; Ehmann, 2005). Smith writes, "Studies have suggested that of all conditions constituting a student's educational experience, their perceptions of assessment systems may have the greatest influence on their activities" (p. 204). When a rubric is handed out to evaluate an assignment, the rubric—advertently or inadvertently—draws students' time, attention, and behavior to the categories with the most points, especially if the rubric is tied to a grade. Ultimately assessment can be a measure of learning but also a shaper of learning (Brown, 1997; Crooks, 1988) and an improver of learning (Gibbs, 1999).

Assessment may interfere or become a barrier to learning, especially if it is tied to grades. Boughton (2008) writes:

> The way to destroy creativity through inappropriate assessment is to structure the art program as a series of directed projects that always receive a grade leaving no possibility for a collection of work to be judged as a record of thinking. If the teacher always chooses the topic, the media, the visual references, the reference sources, the strategy, the style of representation, and the look of the potential outcome where is the opportunity for student interests to be engaged? Why would a student take risks in the search for solutions when he or she knows they will be graded on every project they do? Instead, assessment practices that require thematic study, that do not assess each project, that require evidence of productive risk taking, and demand evidence of sustained independent investigation are more likely to encourage creative output (p. 12-13).

Instead, the assessment process should be an experience where learning is supported, enhanced, and reinforced (Alaska, p. 5). And the Alaska Department of Education cautions that assessment should never rank students (which grading often does) but say whether students have met certain criteria (p. 4).

Another challenge to assessing learning in a creative discipline is tied to the previous two challenges: "what is deemed assessable often becomes what is valued as pedagogically salient in a discipline" (Ross, 1994, p. 2) and in artistic courses of study like dance this is not easy. Ross writes, "Movement as an art form can be chameleonlike" (p. 2), especially when there is no universally accepted pedagogy in the discipline. For example, in dance, technical standards are genre specific and do not cross all styles of dance. The same can be said about newer, computer-based arts fields, where not only is some of the new techniques created in the classroom itself, but the industry and field itself is changing as rapidly as the technology upon which the end-products are created.

And this can create problems with self-assessment, as, after all, self-assessment of perceptual skills on the student's part, not just the facilitator's observations should be a part of the assessment process. This can be tricky because faculty shouldn't judge the assessments based on the student's literary skills (perception in the arts is both a skill of assessment as well as an assessable skill). And this becomes an intractable conundrum in arts assessment: ensuring a student can successfully self-assess his/her own level of creativity. Tonski (2010) questions how faculty can ensure that "a student could successfully self-assess their own level of creativity...It's hard to define stages, or an order, as creativity is always divergent from establish structures" (p.1). And for the most part, universities and colleges never really teach students how to self-assess. Tonski questions if established taxonomies for critical thinking and writing can be adapted to the self-assessment of creative thinking.

Challenges in Logistics and Consistency

Other issues in assessing the aesthetic can be categorized as challenges in logistics and consistency. The most powerful assessment technique and one of the most common in arts disciplines is when reviews are conducted by master-teachers or experts in the field, who either come to campus or to some off-site location (a competition or a performance, perhaps) and the students' works are reviewed by committees of experts outside the classroom setting. This is typical in design and arts competitions; musical performances, master classes, and competitions; and dance and drama programs. Almost every arts field has similar evaluations by experts, and these evaluations present challenges in making sure everyone is present for the event; and everyone understands, agrees upon, and adheres to the evaluation standards. Personal preferences and biases may come into play here, but usually no more than with faculty who possess a familiarity with their students and understand their efforts, challenges, and outlooks that may influence grading and assessment.

Having outside experts as the assessors could have changed the experience of one design student, as quoted by Smith (2013):

> I feel that a lot of my projects turned into what my professors wanted because I felt I wouldn't be able to get the grade I deserved, or that they thought I would get, if I didn't choose like the textile they liked or something, versus a textile I liked…I mean it has like a little bit of me in my projects, but I think it has more of the professors than anything else (p. 210).

Smith says students sometimes think that completing assignments is like playing a game, "which may divert attention from more fundamental learning experiences" (p. 210). Having experts who are strangers except by reputation assess student work also gives students an idea of what it is like post-university. After all, in the workforce, grades are not given and effort is not rewarded; delivering results is the objective. Or as Tonski (2010) writes, "No one's going to see a performance or buy a piece of art because someone worked hard on it" (p. 2).

Tied to who should do some of the assessment is when the assessment is done, as discussed more thoroughly in the Dimensions and Continua of Assessment chapter. The point of time in which we choose to assess sometimes has no or a negative effect on the student (i.e. critique returned after senior project is turned in with no opportunity for changes or incorporating what is learned from the critique into the project). If assessment is to be a tool from which the student can learn and one in which the department or program or university can learn, then the process needs to be built into the curriculum and done throughout the curriculum. Smith (2013) suggests that in the course of long studio projects, "corrective feedback (unaccompanied by grades) may need to be given at more regular intervals" (p. 212).

And lastly, if assessment is done by students, faculty, and experts outside of the academy, it is important that the process be integrated so that the critique and assessment is not seen as ad hoc. For effective assessment in artistic disciplines, the assessment process must employ a variety of techniques in a number of settings, and each of these assessment techniques "is meaningful only when linked to clearly defined purposes. There is no general-purpose formula for assessment that is useful in every setting" (Alaska, 2013, p. 3).

Boughton (2008) writes, "Failure to distinguish between standards and standardization in the practice of assessing art destroys the likelihood that students will experience the curricular conditions necessary to stimulate creative thought. It is time to move back towards a more rational relationship between the creative outcomes we desire and the methods we use to assess it."

Most importantly, faculty, administration, and students all need to understand what is being assessed and why for the assessment process to be successful.

Summary

Understanding the challenges to assessing the aesthetic is the first part of overcoming obstacles to and in the assessment process. Challenges include getting all colleagues onboard the assessment train; narrowing down what to assess and why and then creating an assessment plan that is meaning, manageable, and sustainable that is separate from student grades or rankings; how to integrate outside experts into the assessment process; and making the process just that: a *process* integrated with the curriculum and student learning outcomes.

Also by exploring the challenges in assessment we acknowledge that "Each source [of assessment] has its own biases, and each information-gathering technique has its own strengths and weaknesses. When information obtained by various means is combined or considered collectively, weaknesses in the various methodologies tend to cancel each other, and the assessor can have greater confidence in the results" (Alaska, 2013, p. 4).

References

Attribute, n. (1999) Merriam-Webster's Collegiate Dictionary. Tenth Edition, Springfield, MA: Merriam-Webster, Inc. p. 75.

Alaska Department of Education & Early Development Arts Framework, Chapter 5: Assessment. (2013) Retrieved from http://www.educ.state.ak.us/tls/frameworks/arts/6assess1.htm

Boughton, D. (2008). Promoting creativity in the art class through assessment. Retrieved from http://www.niu.edu/assessment/committees/CAN/PresentationsPapersArticles/boughton-2008.pdf

Brown, G. (1997). *Assessing student learning in higher education.* London: Routledge.

Cohen, R. (2013). *Theatre*. New York, NY:McGraw-Hill Humanities.

Crooks, T.J. (1988). The impact of classroom evaluation practices on students. *Review of Educational Research.* 15(3), p 438-81.

Ehmann, D. (2005). Using assessment to engage graphic design students in their learning experience. Paper presented at Making a Difference: 2005 Evaluations and Assessment Conference, Sydney, 30 November-1 December.

Eisner, E. (1993). Reshaping assessment in education: some criteria in search of practice. *Journal of Curriculum Studies* 25(3), p. 219-33.

Gibbs, G. (1999). Using assessment strategically to change the way students learn, in S. Brown & A. Glasner (Eds) *Assessment Matters in Higher Education: Choosing and Using Diverse Approaches.* Buckingham, England: SRHE and Open University Press, p. 41-53.

Johnson R., Gould. C. (Spring 2009). Special challenges of assessing undergraduate research in the arts and humanities. *CUR Quarterly*, 29 (3), 33-38.

Radocy R., Boyle J. (1987). *Measurement and evaluation of musical experiences.* New York, NY: Schirmer Books.

Ross, J. (1994). The right moves: challenges of dance assessment. *Arts Education Policy Review* 96(1), 11-16.

Smith, K. (2013). Assessment as a barrier in developing design expertise: interior design student perceptions of meanings and sources of grades. *International Journal of Art and Design Education*, 32(2), 203-214.

Skill, N. Webster's Online Dictionary. Retrieved from http://dictionary.reference.com/browse/skill?s=t

Tonski, J. (2010) Intractable conundrums in arts assessment. Retrieved from http://www.units.miamioh.edu/celt/faculty/outcomes/Arts-Assessment/final%20report%20spr%202011.pdf.

Chapter 7: Where to Start Your Assessment: Technical Foundations

'Cheshire Puss,' she began, rather timidly, as she did not at all know whether it would like the name: however, it only grinned a little wider. 'Come, it's pleased so far,' thought Alice, and she went on. 'Would you tell me, please, which way I ought to go from here?' 'That depends a good deal on where you want to get to,' said the Cat. 'I don't much care where--' said Alice. 'Then it doesn't matter which way you go,' said the Cat.
— Lewis Carroll, *Alice in Wonderland*

As readers will have gathered from previous chapters, developing a basic assessment philosophy, a plan, statements of expectations for student learning/student learning outcomes, and a shared understanding of how assessment information will be used are all important prerequisites for selecting appropriate assessment methods. Gathering useful, informal feedback on the effectiveness of a particular instructional strategy may suit the needs of a particular instructor; having more developed systems in place is needed to understand how best to link courses together to achieve student learning outcomes. Having a rigorous, multifaceted, and longitudinal assessment system in place is a basic requirement for accreditation reviews. But at the most basic level, we need to understand where we want to go before we trod the path of selecting assessment methods. That means that we have to define those learning outcomes that we want to see manifest in our students. What expertise should our students achieve? What decisions does such achievement require of us as faculty? How should we best determine what those decisions are, and develop rubrics and other tools to facilitate the success of our students? How do we construct meaningful assessment that takes into account ascending levels of student expertise and accomplishment?

    This chapter addresses the development of student learning outcomes, advances a simple taxonomy of assessment methods appropriate to creative disciplines, provides a review of what methods may be appropriate and in what curricular opportunities, details a list of criteria that may aid the process of selecting appropriate methods, and includes examples of tools relevant to assessment. The chapter concludes with a discussion of assessment in the online environment for creative disciplines.

Assessment Methods: Fundamentals of Relationships and Pattern Recognition

Ultimately assessment is as much about understanding relationships as it is about achievement: between professor and student; between student and art making; among multiple students; among a single professor and her/his relationship to the work of multiple students; and among multiple professors in their collective articulation of art making and in their collective relationship to the creations of their students. It is about being able to discern and differentiate relationships, to articulate relationships, to clarify and to strengthen those relationships. Assessment in creative disciplines also has a great deal to do with pattern recognition at multiple levels. As Popova (2011) notes, "The idea is that in order for us to truly create and contribute to the world, we have to be able to connect countless dots, to cross-pollinate ideas from a wealth of disciplines, to combine and recombine these pieces and build new castles." Ultimately it is about developing an understanding of meta-pattern recognition, across students, across assignments, and across courses that constitute a cohesive program of study. Daniel Pink calls this ability 'symphony', or the ability to grasp the relationship between relationships. He says, "This ability goes by many names -- systems thinking, gestalt thinking, holistic thinking. I prefer to think of it as simply seeing the big picture" (2005, p. 141). The best assessment methods are those that enable us to connect the dots, recognize patterns of achievement or non-achievement across our students, and make adjustments to facilitate their learning.

Student Learning Outcomes in a Tasteful Context...

Most faculty have accrued over the years a deep understanding of how to connect the dots and recognize achievement patterns (or lack thereof!) in students, and frequently this understanding is tacit or nonverbal – faculty have just not been asked to articulate it before. Having conceptual anchors or guides is a highly valuable strategy for connecting the dots and recognizing patterns of achievement in student learning, and articulating them in a way that can be shared with other faculty, students, practicing professionals, and others. If good taste will allow, one way to begin thinking about how to articulate our understanding and develop those conceptual anchors or guides, which we refer to as student learning outcomes, begins with a classic staple of the culinary arts – the apple pie.

Photo 7.1: Apple pie.
Source: Len Rizzi (1990)

Most of us have developed over the years a tacit understanding of what constitutes quality in terms of an apple pie. The first step for us is to surface and articulate those expectations we have – what makes an apple pie good? Next, we would want to think about what kind of gradients or degrees of quality would be appropriate for each of the pie expectations we have articulated. We would want to think through those methods we commonly use to ascertain the extent to which the pie lives up to our expectations, and those points in time in the preparation and baking cycle when it might be useful to check. Finally, it's important to think through the criteria we hold for success in the creation of a quality apple pie. Let's try it!

- What is one criterion for a good apple pie? Among others, a useful criterion might be that the pie is baked all the way through. Nobody likes a gooey pie!
- How might we be able to tell if the pie is baked all the way through? We could use a direct method such as how it tastes. We could also use an indirect method such as the color of the crust. But with just an indirect method, we might come to an errant conclusion without further evidence. For instance, we can get a golden crust on a pie if we put it in an oven at high temperature and quickly brown the outside. But inside the pie would still be raw. So we need multiple methods to make sure the pie is truly baked all the way through.
- In thinking through the baking cycle, when would be the best time to conduct our assessments? For the taste test, we would have to wait until the end of the baking cycle. For the indirect assessment, the crust color, we might check during the baking cycle – thus this would constitute an in-process measurement of pie quality.
- Once we have taken the pie out of the oven, how would we determine the success of the apple pie? Again, we might use a direct method, such

- as the first bite melting in the mouth or the amazing smell of the fresh-baked pie. As an indirect measurement, we might use the rate at which the pie disappears from the pie pan as appreciative onlookers indulge.
- We might get feedback on the cinnamon, the crispness of the apples, the raisins if we used them, the flakiness of the crust, and other facets of the pie. We could use that feedback to make adjustments in the next baking cycle.

As we transition the 'apple pie method' from the culinary arts to other creative disciplines, the same steps may be followed as we did to develop and articulate our criteria for successful apple pie outcomes, develop direct and indirect methods to ascertain quality, think through when it may best serve our interests to conduct assessments, and ultimately determine the success of the pie. To make this transition, we should first think in terms of end results. What do faculty members expect students to learn in a given program of study? Next, we should think through and align our process. How can the faculty structure a curriculum to address those expectations for learning? We will need to consider ways to evaluate expectations: how will faculty know if expectations are met? When would evidence be collected and reviewed? What level of performance do faculty members think meets their standards? How will results be shared? With whom? For what purpose? How will results be used? To apply the apple pie method of articulating and assessing outcomes, let us turn to an example, in this case a student learning outcome from a Master's in Music Composition program.

- **Learning Outcome**: Master's composition graduates will successfully synthesize the musical language of 20th Century composers in their work.
- **Some possible sources of evidence**: student portfolios, course portfolios which include student work
- **Possible ways to measure**: three faculty raters use a simple rubric designed for this purpose to rate student work; panel of judges rates student compositions in live performances.
- **When to Measure**: end of first year; master's performance of their works at end of second year.
- **Possible Standard for Success**: successful synthesis (defined in rubric) of harmonic, rhythmic, formal and scalar materials into student's compositional vocabulary. Evidence may include student work from selected courses, culminating experiences (e.g., exam/performance, composition portfolio).
- **Possible Uses of Results**: an instructor redesigns an assignment, the faculty restructures the sequencing of courses, perhaps adding a new course; the dean allocates resources for course software, or perhaps for a new faculty line.

Taxonomy of Assessment Methods

We have already introduced the notions of direct and indirect assessment methods. From there, a taxonomy of assessment methods is easily articulated. Three basic genres exist.

- **Direct assessment** is assessment that is based on professional judgment, guided by a decision facilitation tool, such as a rubric, that enables us to render similarly and well-informed judgments across situations, across students, and across time. The great majority of assessment in creative disciplines will of necessity be direct assessment, since we typically directly observe the student's works, performances, or designs.
- **Indirect assessment** is the collection of non-observational data about student learning. It consists of reporting about learning, attitudes, or perceptions of learning, but not a direct demonstration of competence. Secondary evidence of learning, such as admission to a professional society, also falls in this category. Indirect assessment includes survey research methods, where students and alumni self-rate, indicate their satisfaction, or give an opinion relative to their education. Graduating student surveys, alumni surveys, and satisfaction surveys are examples of this genre.
- **Unobtrusive or passive assessment** takes several forms. Information derived from student records, usually analyzed by an institutional research office, constitutes an important facet in that important proxies for student learning, such as retention and graduation studies, are vital to effective program management. Unobtrusive or passive assessment is also relevant to assessment in creative disciplines where content is delivered online, since each and every action a student takes in an online course is recorded and may be combined (triangulated) with other direct and indirect assessment methods to form a more complete picture of student learning in the online context.

Using Multiple Methods in Assessment

As articulated above in the apple pie method discussion, when selecting or designing assessment methods, it is generally far preferable to develop an assessment schema that relies upon two or more methods, in order to examine the congruence or areas of agreement among various assessments and come to more robust, replicable decisions about the meaning of assessment findings. Additionally, many advocate the use of a mixed-methods approach to assessment (direct and indirect methods; perhaps unobtrusive methods as well). This may be represented in triangular fashion (Hoey, Marr, and Gardner, 2002), as in Figure 7.1 below.

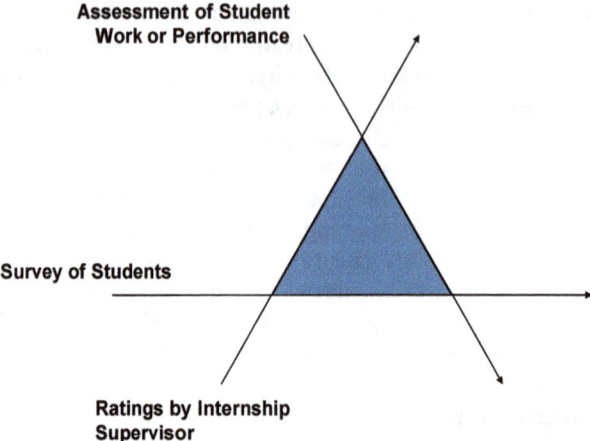

Figure 7.1. Triangulation of Assessment Methods
Source: Adapted from Hoey, Marr and Gardner (2002)

As long as the directionality of the results is similar (represented by the arrows for assessment of student performance, survey of students, and ratings by internship supervisor) and there exists conceptual overlap in the content or area being assessed (represented by the dark blue triangular area), in situations where multiple methods are used together the results are in general substantially more useful in clarifying needs for adjustments based on assessment data collected.

Embedded, Objective, and External Assessment

Assessment methods may also be thought of as being (1) embedded within the course or curriculum, such as end of term performance juries, exams, portfolios, studio critiques, etc., (2) objective in nature and not necessarily a part of expected student work, such as standardized testing, or (3) external to the curriculum, such as might be provided by internship directors, competition juries, or co-op supervisors.

An example of an embedded curricular assessment is given below – a performance assessment check sheet for junior Theatre majors at Winthrop University, using end of term juried performances as the opportunity to assess student competence. As an assessment tool, it has both inherent advantages and limitations. In terms of advantages, the check sheet clearly concentrates on four important competency areas for Theatre – acting ability, communication skills, movement, and stage presence. The form includes space for open-ended commentary on each competency area; students are assessed on a five-point scale on each dimension, with 5 being the highest rating and 1 being the lowest. The form can be filled out quickly and easily by faculty, comments added, and both the ratings and the comments may be summarized across students to determine areas of strength in student performances and opportunities for bolstering student achievement where a number of students did not demonstrate adequate competency. Limitations include that no information is provided to more closely describe what each rating scale degree means for each competency area, thus coming to agreement among faculty as to what a "3" or a "4" means on the communications skills competency rating may be difficult to achieve. Also, since no information is provided on what each scale degree means, students may not be clear on the feedback they are receiving. This lack of more precise information may be addressed in the open ended commentary, provided all faculty members reviewing the performance write in evaluative commentary and feedback that addresses each of the competencies.

Winthrop University Department of Theatre and Dance
JUNIOR ASSESSMENT CHECK SHEET FOR EVALUATING THEATRE STUDENT PERFORMANCES

Student Name_____ Date _____

I ACTING ABILITY (i.e. emotional accessibility and believability). The actor demonstrates believability in their acting choices. The actor is connected to the character's emotional world. The actor is connected to the needs of the character.

Rating: 5   4   3   2   1
Comments:

II COMMUNICATION SKILLS (i.e. vocalization and articulation) the actor must articulate well, make the material audible and understandable, and use healthy vocal technique as required by the material.

Rating: 5   4   3   2   1
Comments:

III MOVEMENT (i.e. physicalization) the actor has made strong choices about the physical life of the character as required by the material. Use of the available acting space, gestures, etc. should grow organically out of the actor's performance.

Rating: 5   4   3   2   1
Comments:

IV STAGE PRESENCE (i.e. personal and professional comportment). You are looking for professional attitude and comportment from the actor. This includes behavior and dress that would work favorably for them in a professional audition situation. For example, do they appear nervous? Did they fumble lines? How well do they conduct their introduction, conclusion, work, relationship to you? Do they exude confidence and a strong stage persona? And most important, are they responsibly prepared?

Rating: 5   4   3   2   1

Comments:

ASSESSMENT SCORING KEY					
5	4	3	2	1
Excellent		Average		Poor

Figure 7.2: Theatre performance check sheet
Source: Adapted from Winthrop University Department of Theatre and Dance (n.d.)

A more fully developed, rubric-based performance assessment schema is offered by Barlow (2013). It is instructive to compare this approach to assessing student performance in theatre to the one given above. The usage of more highly-detailed rubrics (and underlying definitions) offers the distinct possibility of a higher degree of consistency among raters. Very important to note is that Barlow's (2013) assessment schema involves the creation of a series of rubrics, keyed to the expected level of competencies that students would be expected to have acquired by a certain point in their programs of study. We might call this a developmental approach to rubric-based assessment. Shown below is the rubric that corresponds to Level 6, or third-year student performance, in the BA (Honors) program in Theatre Arts at Southampton Solent University; not displayed are similar rubrics developed for Level 5 (second-year) and Level 4 (first-year) performance assessments in the three-year program. The importance of such an approach to assessment in creative disciplines can scarcely be overstated, since a core element of mastery teaching in the discipline is to know what to expect, what to look for, and how to communicate what level of competence is expected to each of our students.

Table 7.3: BA in theatre performance rubric

Dimensions	A 1 and 2	A 3 and 4	B	C	D	F 1-4
CRAFTSMAN-SHIP IN PERFORM-ANCE (Technical Skills)	Consistently demonstrates the highest level of technical competence in use of body, voice, listening, reaction and related performance skills. Fully engaged in process. Demonstrates ability to use technology of medium to the highest degree to support performance.	The use of body, voice listening, reaction and related performance skills is consistently competent and indicates mastery in some areas. Performer is fully engaged in process and demonstrates full understanding of the capabilities of supporting technology.	The use of body, voice listening, reaction and related performance skills is competent throughout and indicates more developed ability in some areas. Performer is engaged in process and is aware of supporting technology with many areas of strength.	The use of body, voice listening, reaction and related performance skills is basically competent and shows a more developed capability in one area. Performer is engaged in the process. Use of technology is satisfactory.	The use of body, voice listening, reaction and related performance skills is adequate. Performer is engaged in process. Use of technology is adequate though limited.	The use of body, voice listening, reaction and related performance skills is inadequate and lacks basic competence. Inadequate levels of engagement in process. One or more technical areas of artefact are unsatisfactory.

WHERE TO START YOUR ASSESSMENT

PREPARATION & REHEARSAL	Candidate(s) takes advantage of all resources available with high-order, independent research, preparation &learning of text. Work demonstrates considerable initiative. Work evidences advanced team-working.	Candidate(s) makes full use of all resources available and demonstrates high levels of research, preparation & learning of text. Work demonstrates some initiative. Work evidences excellent levels of team-working.	Candidate(s) takes advantage of all resources available with evidence of research, preparation & learning of text. Work demonstrates some initiative. Work evidences a high level of team-working.	Candidate(s) takes advantage of resources available and work indicates satisfactory research, preparation & learning of text. Work demonstrates satisfactory levels of independence. Work evidences team-working.	Candidate(s) takes advantage of resources available. Work demonstrates adequate levels of research, preparation & learning of text . Work demonstrates adequate levels of independence. Limited evidence of team-working	Candidate(s) fails to take advantage of all resources available. Inadequate research, preparation & learning of text . Work demonstrates insufficient independence. Underdeveloped team-working.
CHARACTER-ISATION SKILLS	Highest levels of character detail in construction of performance. Characterisation demonstrates critical reflection and insight. Level of ability to sustain this in performance is significantly beyond the expectations for this level.	High levels of character detail in construction of performance. Characterisation demonstrates critical reflection and insight. Level of ability to sustain this in performance surpasses the expectations for this level	Highest levels of, character detail in construction of performance. Characterisation demonstrates good levels of critical reflection and insight. Level of ability to sustain this in performance reflects the expectations for this level.	Acceptable levels of, character detail in construction of performance. Characterisation demonstrates adequate levels of critical reflection and insight. Level of ability to sustain this in performance meets the expectations for this level	Consistent level of, character detail in construction of performance. Characterisation demonstrates some critical reflection and insight. Level of ability to sustain this in performance is adequate for this level.	Inadequate levels of, character detail in construction of performance. Characterisation lacks critical reflection and insight. Insufficient ability to sustain a consistent level in performance.
ANALYTICAL SKILLS	Performance reflects highest level understanding of relationship of form to content. Displays originality and exemplary aesthetic, commercial or intellectual underpinning. Demonstrates highly developed understanding of professional contexts and expectations.	Performance reflects high level understanding of relationship of form to content. Displays originality and superior aesthetic, commercial or intellectual underpinning with developed understanding of	Performance reflects thorough level understanding of relationship of form to content. Displays good aesthetic, commercial or intellectual underpinning with clear understanding of professional contexts	Performance reflects appropriate level understanding of relationship of form to content. Displays sound aesthetic, commercial or intellectual underpinning with some understanding of professional contexts	Performance reflects adequate level understanding of relationship of form to content. Displays some aesthetic, commercial or intellectual underpinning and limited understanding of professional	Performance reflects inadequate understanding of relationship of form to content. Displays no aesthetic, commercial or intellectual underpinning with underdeveloped understanding of professional contexts

			professional contexts and expectations.	and expectations.	and expectations.	contexts and expectations.	and expectations.
CREATIVITY	Performance demonstrates creative ambition, originality, execution and professionalism which is beyond the expectations for undergraduate work.	Performance demonstrates high levels of creative ambition, execution and professionalism which is beyond the expectations for this level.	Performance demonstrates considerable creative ambition, execution and professionalism appropriate for this level.	Performance demonstrates satisfactory creative ambition, execution and professionalism for this level.	Performance demonstrates adequate creative ambition, execution and professionalism for this level.	Performance demonstrates lack of creative ambition, execution and professionalism for this level.

CRAFTSMAN SHIP IN PERFORMANCE: This reflects the tutors' ability to see the student's application of the vocal and physical techniques learned during training to the creation of character or differentiation between a range of characters where multiple roles are played in a production. The tutor's judgement will also be applied to the student's ability to be committed to their performance and fully engaged in listening and responding naturally to other performers in the context of the script. In screen projects a judgement will be made on the student's ability to adapt their performance to the technical demands of the medium, making their characterisation clear in relation to the camera and sound recording.

PREPERATION AND REHEARSAL: It may be expected that student's will arrive at the beginning of the rehearsal period for a Stage or Screen production having learned all their lines from the script. Even if this is not the case, students will be assessed on their application towards researching and developing characterisation. This will include the creation of a biography, writing monologues, identifying all the beats/actions for their character from scene to scene and being able to play their character's objectives from scene to scene as well as being able to identify and act out their character's superobjective for the script as a whole.

CHARACTERISATION SKILLS: This refers to the ability to see the student demonstrating the ability to combine their character research with their Vocal and Physical work into the creation of a consistent characterisation. The student will be expected to sustain characterisation in performance as well as reflecting on the experience of each performance to improve their performances during the run of the production.

ANALYTICAL SKILLS: This refers to the student's ability to demonstrate an understanding of the context within which they are working, whether it be in relation to the form or the genre within which they are working or other stylistic considerations. Students should be able to identify and demonstrate the ability work within the different technical as well as commercial imperatives of working for a range of different stage forms (musical, commercial, experimental) as well as television and film methodologies.

CREATIVITY: This demands that the student be able to demonstrate their ability to make synergistic links of all of the above in the execution of their work. Students will be expected to demonstrate their commitment to and ability to rehearse and perform in a proactive fashion, supplying imaginative ideas/suggestions to their performance work and demonstrating an understanding of how high levels of application and commitment add to the development of professionalism and therefore employability.

Source: Barlow (2013).

Objective or Standardized Assessments

Typically undertaken as part of a larger accountability mandate within a single university or university system, objective assessment relies on standardization and accuracy (reliability and validity) of measurement as twin selling points in demonstrating the value added or gains of students through a program of study, in a manner that can be compared across multiple institutions and students, irrespective of institutional mission. Colleges and universities utilize objective assessments for testing general education knowledge (such as reading comprehension, critical thinking skills, and mathematical reasoning skills) in no small part to provide demonstration of student competence in General Education to meet the requirements of state systems and regional accreditation agencies in the United States. Exams such as the College Base, the Collegiate Learning Assessment (CLA), the ETS Proficiency Profile, and the Collegiate Assessment of Academic Proficiency (CAAP) are used for this purpose. Other objective assessments are available for summative assessment of student achievement within the major, such as the Major Field Achievement Tests (MFAT) and Area Concentration Achievement Tests (ACAT), however available options are limited within the creative disciplines. An MFAT for Music History and Theory exists, as well as ACATs for Art History, Design, and Studio Art. The advantages of using standardized assessments include their comparability across institutions and the ability to conduct benchmarking studies at the institution or program level. Disadvantages of standardized assessments include the cost of administration, the potential for lack of fit between what faculty members teach in a program and a particular standardized assessment, and the problem of motivating students to put forth their best efforts in an assessment that is not directly linked to their coursework or program of study. In the case of creative disciplines, standardized assessments are limited to the cognitive domain. The affective and motor skills domains, so important in creative disciplines, are not typically amenable to assessment via standardized methods.

External Assessment

Assessment methods external to the curriculum and to the school or institution itself include various forms of experiential assessment – for example internships, design competitions and charrettes, student co-op experiences, and student or professional competitions. Faculty would expect to see an assessment of the student's professional and workplace skills included in such assessments of student experiential learning opportunities, but important program-level student learning outcomes are also essential to include. Hoey, Marr, and Gardner (2002) noted that in-process external professional assessments and employer-related feedback both provide vital in-process information about student competencies as seen from outside the institution. The example given below from the Interior Design Department at California State University, Sacramento illustrates the inclusion of important learning outcomes such as communication skills and the quality, accuracy and creativity of the materials produced, as well as workplace-related skills.

STUDENT INTERN FINAL EVALUATION   FORM IIIF

Professional
Supervisor: _____   Student Intern: _____
            (Please Print)   (Please Print)

Firm/Agency: _____
                  (Please Print)

This non-confidential form is designed to serve as an integral part of the student's learning experience. It is recommended that the completed evaluation be reviewed/discussed directly with the intern. The Professional Supervisor should complete the Final Evaluation during the 14th week of the internship.. In addition to ratings, comments would be helpful. The student intern is responsible for ensuring that the submission deadline is met; this will entail scheduling a specific meeting with the Professional Supervisor to discuss the Final evaluation.

PROFESSIONAL COMPETENCIES	COMMENTS
Assessment Value: 10=Highest 1=Lowest NA=Not Applicable	

1. **Communication Skills**
   a. Verbal   _____

   b. Written   _____

   c. Graphic   _____

2. **Responsibility**
   a. Promptness   _____

   b. Attendance   _____

   c. Follow-through _____

3. **Ability to work with others (courtesy, judgment, cooperation)**
   a. Professional Supervisor _____

   b. Staff   _____

   c. Client   _____

   d. Reps   _____

   e. Other/Specify _____

4. **Professional awareness of:**
   a. Protocol   _____

   b. Communication channels _____

   c. Design Process _____

Interior Design Internship Handbook

STUDENT INTERN FINAL EVALUATION (Continued) FORM IIIF

5. Self Reliance

a. Ability to adjust to change ______

b. Ability to acquire necessary information ______

c. Ability to learn new methods, skills, and ideas ______

d. Initiative ______

6. Materials produced

(quality, accuracy, creativity)

a. Sample Boards ______

b. Architectural drawings ______

c. Presentation drawings ______

d. Other (specify) ______

7. Note Strengths:

8. Areas in need of improvement:

9. Required Signatures

Professional Supervisor Date Student Date

Interior Design Internship Handbook Page 27

Figure 7.4: Student internship evaluation form.

Source: Adapted from California State University Sacramento Interior Design Internship Handbook (2011).

Direct Assessment Methods in Creative Disciplines

In this section we focus on instruments and approaches that may be used by faculty, groups of faculty, peer reviewers, and professionals to form judgments around student competencies and proficiency through direct observation and evaluation of student work or of student performance. Direct assessment methods are the most popular type of assessment method for creative disciplines. Examples of basic questions we might want to answer through direct assessment include:

- How well are students assimilating tools and techniques within the discipline?
- To what extent and at what level are the students acquiring the knowledge, skills, and abilities that faculty deem appropriate to professional practice?
- How are students developing in the ability to engage in reflective critique and metacognitive development, both within the discipline as well as other coursework?

A direct assessment opportunity is provided within the context of an assignment, performance, portfolio, or some other demonstration of student competency that can be assessed by a suitably qualified faculty member or designate. Direct assessment opportunities abound in creative disciplines. Some common examples include:

- Performance assessments, such as a theatrical, musical, or dance performance
- Portfolios and e-Portfolios
- Externally juried design or performance competitions and charrettes
- Individual and group projects, for example senior studio projects
- Demonstrations and presentations
- Written and oral exams
- Licensure exams (for Interior Design and Architecture, for example)
- Case studies
- Simulations

Depending upon the assignment, the learning outcomes to be assessed, and the context, both rubrics and check sheets are the primary tools for such direct assessment.

Rubrics

Rubrics, as in the Barlow (2013) example above, are scoring tools that disaggregate an expected work, performance, or assignment into component parts. Rubrics are grounded in qualitative descriptions that apply to each competency level and each facet of an intended student learning outcome. For example, in a jury performance rubric for Music Performance we might want to include the basic elements of music. Each competency level is assigned a score which may be summed across an entire rubric and then averaged across students -- both to determine variances in aggregate ratings and to indicate both areas of strength and needs for improvement within the curriculum. Rubrics are not only a primary tool for direct assessment in creative disciplines; they also serve as communication devices to clarify performance expectations for students.

What goes into producing a good rubric? Three elements are necessary: (1) Faculty time, (2) agreement on the elements of a work or performance that taken together constitute a demonstration of expertise, and (3) a willingness to collaboratively calibrate and refine the language used until agreement is reached on the rating of a particular work or performance about 70 percent of the time or more. Rubric development, scoring and calibration are all areas in which a wide literature exists, well beyond the scope of this chapter. For example, Dirlam and Singeisen (2009) describe a rigorous method for developing rubrics in the context of Architecture using an iterative faculty interview technique to identify and validate elements of expertise in the discipline. For the present purposes, a guide to writing good rubrics is most immediately relevant. One of the most popular 'rubrics on rubrics,' or guides in how to construct a rubric, is included below for reference.

Aunt Olive's Rubric on Rubrics

by Ned Miller

	4	3	2	1
Useful	Assessment is useful and convenient to the learner from the beginning of the discussion about the task, and it concentrates all student energy on what is important to accomplish.	Learners can understand the assessment and begin to use it before the task has begun. It focuses their energy on what it is important to accomplish.	Assessment is available to learners at some point before the task is completed. Students can use it to get an idea of what is important to accomplish.	Assessment not available to learner or learner cannot interpret or understand it.
Self-Assess	Learners required to self-assess and are required to reflect and concentrate on quality of work.	Learners encouraged to self-assess and reflect on quality of work.	Learners are invited to self-assess, but may not reflect on quality.	There is no promotion to self-assess or focus on quality.

Descriptors	Has explicit descriptors which allow the instructor to distinctly discriminate within a range of quality. (4 or 6 are ideal so no "middle" exists.)	Has specific descriptors which allow the instructor to discriminate a range of quality which is limited to few enough so that discrimination is distinct (usually 3-7 levels).	Has descriptors which help the instructor measure specific items, but there may be too many items.	No understandable descriptors.
Key Elements	Measures only vital elements which are critical to the task. No items of low consequence.	Measures key elements which are essential to the task. Few items of low consequence.	Meaningful items assessed, but may be of limited significance.	Inappropriate items are assessed (due to ease of grading?).
Valid	An explicit set of objectives is measured. Understanding is a prerequisite to scoring well. Students cannot score well or poorly due to factors unrelated to objectives.	A distinct set of objectives is measured. Students must understand the concepts to score well and will score well if they understand.	Vague objectives may be present. Students who understand objectives tend to score higher.	Students are uncertain as to what is expected. Assessment does not measure what it says it measures.
Reliable	Different instructors grading the same task will get the same results.	Different instructors grading the same task will get highly similar results.	Instructors are guided to similar results.	There is no consistency of results.

Source: http://www.carla.umn.edu/assessment/vac/evaluation/ref_2.html. Reproduced with the author's permission.

Check Sheets

Check sheets, as detailed above in the example from Winthrop University, are also rating forms, but tend to provide less information about the constructs being assessed and no description of what each rating means. Like other assessment methods, their appropriate use depends upon the importance and depth of the assignment, those specific student learning outcomes faculty expect to see demonstrated, the time available for assessment, and other contextual factors.

Indirect Assessment Methods in Creative Disciplines

In this part of the chapter we explore indirect assessment methods – those that produce secondary evidence about student learning, perceptions of student learning, or the results of student learning. Surveys, focus groups, and exit interviews are common indirect methods.

Survey Research

Questionnaire survey research is a long-standing form of indirect assessment in higher education. Traditional survey research formats include in-class and mailed paper and pencil surveys as well as telephone surveys; however, web-based surveys have become the dominant survey format due to their ease of administration and data collection, lower cost, and alignment with student expectations for communication style. For more in-depth information on survey research, readers may be interested in Dillman, Smyth, and Christian (2008), a preeminent and inclusive guide to Internet, mixed-method, and mail survey techniques.

Student orientation surveys, satisfaction surveys, and alumni surveys have long been used for institutional information, such as for establishing ongoing contact with alumni for continuing education and fundraising purposes. More recent is the movement to explicitly align current student, exit, and alumni survey items with important student learning outcomes in program or department-based surveys, or as part of a larger institutional survey. For example, on the Kenyon College Studio Art Program Student Opinion Survey (see http://documents.kenyon.edu/reaccreditation/StudioArtstudentopinionsurvey.pdf), a graduating senior survey, students are asked to rate the influence of the Studio Art Program on their individual development, both as artists and educated persons, in terms of:

- A. The development of your art related ideas
- B. The development of your art related skills
- C. Your ability to evaluate your own work
- D. Your ability to evaluate the work of others
- E. Your ability to speak about art
- F. Your ability to write about art
- G. Your ability to think creatively and solve problems
- H. Your ability to work independently
- I. Your ability to think creatively
- J. Your knowledge of the art world beyond Kenyon

Survey research is also the assessment method of choice for important feedback mechanisms such as alumni surveys to gain information on postgraduate employment, employer satisfaction studies, and supervisor ratings of student internships, as in the example presented above from CSU Sacramento.

Standardized surveys, taken by students across multiple institutions, are also part of the assessment landscape in higher education. For example, the Cooperative Institutional Research Program (CIRP) survey of incoming first-year students, affiliated with the Higher Education Research Institute at UCLA, has been used for decades to help understand incoming student characteristics, values, attitudes, and beliefs.

Important for assessment of arts alumni, the Strategic National Arts Alumni Project (SNAAP, see http://snaap.indiana.edu/) is a carefully developed instrument currently used by over 70 institutions to assess the outcomes of an education in creative disciplines and to enable better connections between careers in the arts and education in creative disciplines. Only in national use since 2011, research from SNAAP has already resulted in meaningful information for education in creative disciplines. For example, Miller and Lambert (2013) report that survey respondents offer a cohesive set of recommendations for faculty to include in creative discipline curricula:

- Incorporate open-ended projects (top skill #1) and group projects (top skill #3)
- Require analysis of theories or reviews/critiques (top skill #5) and provide opportunities for feedback and revision (top skill #2)
- Ensure curricula include a firm knowledge foundation in a wide variety of areas (top skill #4) (Miller and Lambert, 2013, p. 32)

Interviews

Interviews, either telephone or face-to-face, are another popular indirect assessment method. Many departments precede a face-to-face exit interview (for example with a program chair) with a written exit survey from which specific themes may be developed in the context of an exit interview. The face validity of exit interview information is one of its greatest strengths – students who have been through a program of study are more likely to be trusted to be able to report about their experience and learning in the program of study (Hoey and Nault, 2002). A protocol for an exit interview from the Department of Theatre and Dance at Southeast Missouri State University is instructive in this regard (Note: see http://www.semo.edu/theatreanddance/current/exit.htm).

Southeast Missouri State University, Theatre & Dance Experience Exit Interview for Graduating Seniors

The following questions are asked on Southeast's Department of Theatre and Dance exit interview with graduating seniors.

1. Rate your own efforts and accomplishments in your academic work at Southeast Missouri State University on a scale of 1 – 10 (1 = lowest, 10 = highest), and briefly relate at least one specific example of your academic achievements. Include class titles, GPAs, or other specific information that you feel is appropriate.
2. Rate your own efforts and accomplishments in your production participation (Performance & Design/Technical) on a scale of 1 – 10 (1 = lowest, 10 = highest), and briefly relate at least one specific example from those achievements. Include production name(s) and other pertinent information.
3. Briefly recount at least one faculty feedback situation or evaluation that has been most helpful during your career at Southeast, and explain why. Please recommend at least one suggestion.
4. Briefly discuss at least one aspect of each of the following production processes that worked well for you, and suggest at least one recommendation for improvement of each process.
    A. Selection of Productions
    B. Auditions or Production Assignments/Design Process
    C. Rehearsals or Construction
    D. Faculty Mentoring
    E. Performances
5. Briefly discuss a minimum of two plans or possibilities that you have for yourself after graduation.
6. Do the same for your professional goals in the future.
7. Briefly discuss two ways in which your Southeast training has prepared you to achieve your future goals.
8. Please share at least two constructive suggestions for improving the Southeast undergraduate theatre and dance programs.
9. How may the department reach you in the future? Please provide us with your permanent mailing address, permanent telephone, and e-mail.

Figure 7.5: Exit interview questions
Source: Southeast Missouri State University, Department of Theatre and Dance (n.d.)

Focus Groups

Focus groups are a useful qualitative research technique in situations where it is important to gain insights on those opinions, beliefs, attitudes, or perceptions that a stakeholder group – for example faculty, students, alumni, or employers – hold about a phenomenon of interest (Greenbaum, 1997; Hoey and Nault, 2002). Focus groups are a moderator-led, dialogue-based method of gathering input and opinions in a synergistic manner, where the sum of the interactive group dialogue is more than could be expected from individual interviews. In assessment within creative disciplines, focus groups might be used to gather employer or alumni input about a new program of study or specialization in one of the creative disciplines, to gain insights from an advisory group concerning perceptions of program currency in the discipline, or to elicit input from students concerning their experience in a design competition.

Unobtrusive or Passive Methods in Assessment

Unobtrusive or passive assessment takes several forms. Information derived from student records constitutes an essential facet in that important proxies for student learning such as retention and graduation studies are vital to effective program management. Unobtrusive or passive assessment is also relevant to assessment in creative disciplines where content is delivered online. While most student work submitted in an online course may be assessed online using direct methods, the interactions students have with technology produces evidence of their engagement with content—time spent on a website, time spent with a particular online text, number of articles accessed online and similar measures are passively recorded, can be collected and analyzed, and then used for assessment purposes with other direct and indirect methods or the signs and traces of student learning. This aspect of unobtrusive/passive assessment is further detailed below in the section on online assessment methods.

Information from Student Records

Program-level information on student retention, progression through a course of study, transfer in or departure from a program, time to degree, and graduation rates are not strictly speaking assessment of student learning, yet those measures function as vital managerial proxies for such learning and for the health of a program overall. An office of institutional research is usually responsible for producing studies using institutional data on topics such as retention or graduation by program. Frequently used in periodic academic program reviews, information from student records may be disaggregated and viewed across multiple years; it may be benchmarked against similar information from a school, college or university overall; or in the case of a data sharing consortium, may be part of a multiple-institution comparison. The Association for Institutional Research, https://www.airweb.org/pages/default.aspx, provides numerous resources for studies involving institutional data.

Information from Agency Files

For creative disciplines such as Architecture and Interior Design where professional licensure is an important outcome, utilizing disaggregated information on student performance in each subsection of a set of licensure exam results may be a key student learning assessment strategy. An analysis of section-by-section licensure exam results permits faculty to compare those results to how and where content is distributed within a program of study, and to map out any needed adjustments to effect improvements in future licensure exam performance.

Increasingly, the United States Department of Education and state-level agencies are demanding professional placement and employment information of college and university program graduates as an accountability measure, as career-oriented national accreditation agencies have been doing for some time. Alumni surveys have previously been used for this purpose, but state-level agencies are also matching data on graduating students in public institutions with state employment files to obtain approximate information on professional positions and salaries of graduates. This trend, impractical and less than relevant for many creative disciplines as it is, can be expected to continue.

Selecting Assessment Methods

Given the wide variety of assessment methods available, it can seem a daunting task to select and/or develop an appropriate set of assessment methods that map well to student learning outcomes. Selecting and developing assessment methods is a task best undertaken as a collaborative activity by faculty within a department or program. Consideration of the timing and sequence of assessments in a course or curriculum, their relationship to course and program-level student learning outcomes, and how they may be used together to form a triangulated view of student acquisition of competence are all important. As a brief guide, below are a number of questions that faculty may want to use to help steer the selection process:

- **Relevant**: Does the method offer a good fit or match to the course or curriculum?
- **Useful**: does the method provide useful course and program-level information, appropriate to the degree level?
- **Feedback**: Can the method be used to provide cogent feedback to students that will aid their understanding?
- **Trustworthy**: Is the method sufficiently vetted and robust that it produces trustworthy information?
- **Understandable**: Can the assessment results obtained be readily understood by multiple users?
- **Technical quality**: Does the method produce information that is considered valid and reliable within the norms of qualitative or quantitative analysis?
- **Time involved**: Will the method require a long period of development or preparation?
- **Costs and benefits**: What are the direct and indirect costs of using a particular approach? Are those costs justified by the expected benefits?
- **Useful to the students**: Will students perceive the assessment to be of value towards their learning, and will they cooperate?
- **Fairness**: Is the method a fair procedure, or does it introduce bias?
- **Protection of human subjects**: Does the assessment method afford reasonable protections to students? If assessment information obtained is intended to be used for research and publication purposes, are informed consent procedures in place?

To come to clear decisions about what assessment methods to use, lining assessment methods up in a columnar format is one way to determine the strengths and weaknesses of one method compared to another. The example below illustrates (in an abbreviated form) how this might be done. To ensure that such a comparison is relevant, the student learning outcome to be assessed and the context in terms of time, manner, and place within the curriculum should be stated. Note that scores are for example only and are not intended to be a value judgment of any particular method.

Table 7.5: Sample matrix for comparison of assessment methods.

Student Learning Outcome Assessed: Students will utilize appropriate technology in the creation and study of art.			
Time, Manner, and Place in the Curriculum: Senior studio project, taken near or at the culmination of the degree program			
Selection Criteria	Method 1: Rubric-based project assessment by panel of faculty	Method 2: Internship Supervisor Feedback	Method 3: Focus group of student perceptions
	Scoring Key: 5 = highest rating; 1 = lowest rating		
Relevant	5	1	2
Useful	5	2	3
Trustworthy	5	4	4
Technical Quality	5	5	4
Etc.	-	-	-
Total Score	20	12	13

Summary

This chapter has addressed the development of student learning outcomes first through a discussion of pattern recognition and then through application of the 'apple pie' method. The chapter moved on to delineate a simple taxonomy of assessment methods appropriate to creative disciplines consisting of direct, indirect, and unobtrusive or passive methods, the latter being more useful in the online context than in on-ground programs. Within each area of the taxonomy, appropriate methods have been presented and examples provided, as well as references for further resources. The chapter provided suggestions on how to select assessment methods, and concluded with a discussion of assessment in the online environment for creative disciplines.

Based on the student learning outcomes we as faculty deem appropriate for our students in their progress towards mastery in the discipline, we select appropriate assessment methods. Planning out our assessments and creating a structure or schema for our assessment endeavors will help ensure success. There are many considerations to take into account in the assessment planning process, and this topic is dealt with at length in the following chapter.

References

Barlow, J. (2013). Level 6 rubric: Production. Year 3, BA (Hons.) program in Theatre Performance, Southampton Solent University. Used by permission of author.

Carroll, Lewis (2003, original edition 1865). *Alice's Adventures in Wonderland.* New York: Little Simon, 2003.

Department of Interior Design, California State University Sacramento (2011). Student Intern Final Evaluation. In *California State University Interior Design Internship Handbook,* pages 26-27. Retrieved from http://www.al.csus.edu/design/forms/internship_handbook_fall_2011.pdf.

Department of Theatre and Dance, Southeast Missouri State University (n.d.). Exit interview for graduating seniors. Retrieved from http://www.semo.edu/theatreanddance/current/exit.htm.

Dillman, D., Smyth, J. , and Christian, L. *Internet, Mail, and Mixed-Mode Surveys: The Tailored Design Method* (3rd Edition). Hoboken, NJ: John Wiley & Sons, 2008.

Dirlam, D. K. and Singeisen, S. R. (2009). Collaboratively Crafting a UniqueArchitecture Education through MODEL Assessment. In P. Crisman and M. Gillem (Eds.) *The Value of Design* (pp. 445-455), Washington, DC: ACSA Publishing.

Ewell, P. (1984). *The self-regarding institution: information for excellence.* Boulder, CO: National Center for Higher Education Management Systems.

Gibson, D. and Webb, M. (2013). Working Group 5: Assessment as, for and of 21st century learning. Paper presented at EDUsummIT 2013, Washington, D.C., October 1-2, 2013. Retrieved 9/15/2013 from http://www.edusummit.nl/fileadmin/contentelementen/kennisnet/EDUSummIT/Documenten/2013/Pre-summit_brief_paper_TWG5_-_Assessment.pdf.

Greenbaum, T. *The Handbook for Focus Group Research* (2nd Edition). Thousand Oaks, CA: Sage Publications, 1997.

Hoey, J., Marr, J., and Gardner, D. (2002). Multiple Vantage Points for Employment - Related Feedback: Some Results. Paper presented at 2nd National Conference on Outcomes Assessment, 2002 ABET Annual Meeting, Pittsburgh, PA, October 31, 2002.

Hoey, J. and Nault, E. (2002). Trust: The Missing Ingredient in Assessment. *International Journal of Engineering Education*, Vol. 18, No. 2, pp. 117-127.

Kenyon College (n.d.). Studio Art Program Student Opinion Survey. Retrieved from http://documents.kenyon.edu/reaccreditation/StudioArtstudentopinionsurvey.pdf.

Miller, N. (n.d.). Aunt Olive's Rubric on Rubrics. Retrieved from http://www.carla.umn.edu/assessment/vac/evaluation/ref_2.html.

Miller, A. and Lambert, A. (2013). Best Practices in Using Alumni Data for Arts Program Assessment. Presentation at the Assessment in the Arts Conference, Denver, CO, July 2013.

Moore, M. (1989). Editorial: Three types of interaction. *The American Journal of Distance Education,* 3(2), 1-7.

Pink, D. (2005). *A Whole New Mind.* New York: Riverhead Books.

Popova, M. (2011, May). Networked Knowledge and Combinatorial Creativity. Retrieved from http://www.brainpickings.org/index.php/2011/08/01/networked-knowledge-combinatorial-creativity/.

Shute, V. J. (2011). Stealth assessment in computer-based games to support learning. In S. Tobias & J. D. Fletcher (Eds.), *Computer games and instruction* (pp. 503-524). Charlotte, NC: Information Age Publishers.

Suskie, L. (2004). Assessing Student Learning: A Common Sense Guide. New York: Wiley.

Chapter 8: Online Assessment in Creative Disciplines

It ought to be remembered that there is nothing more difficult to take in hand, more perilous to conduct, or more uncertain in its success, than to take the lead in the introduction of a new order of things. Because the innovator has for enemies all those who have done well under the old conditions and lukewarm defenders in those who may do well under the new.
—Machiavelli, *The Prince* (1513)

Online learning has grown exponentially over the last two decades in higher education, also bringing with it advances in online assessment (or e-Assessment). While programs in creative disciplines have not been as quick to adapt to the online environment as programs in liberal arts, business, and education, the trend towards established institutions offering online degree programs in creative disciplines is unmistakable. Developments in information technology have been a critical enabler of assessment for online, blended, and strictly classroom-based programs. Advances in computational and graphics card memory, software with superb object visualization and 3-dimensional rotation capabilities, screen color resolution that offers pixilation beyond the perceptual boundaries of even the most discriminating color theorist, the emergence of social media tribes, the ubiquitous use of blogs on creativity and creative disciplines, and collaborative text- and video-conferencing applications have all played a role in overcoming practical and technological barriers that hitherto precluded the widespread advance of online offerings in creative disciplines. Without sacrificing the need for face-to-face interaction that characterizes so many creative programs, a number of institutions have moved to offering either wholly online or blended learning programs that include limited residency requirements to supplement regular submission and assessment of creative works online. It is fair to say that taking creative programs online results in the need for some fundamental changes in our approach to pedagogy – from constant and direct observer of our students' work to guide, coach, and facilitator of our students' growth in the discipline. In this chapter we focus on questions of what to assess in the online context and assessment tools that are useful in online environments, understanding that a number of the tools discussed might equally be applied to classroom-based and blended learning environments. The chapter includes an in-depth look at the multiple cultural and political considerations, desirable feature sets, and questions to ask at the strategic, operational, and tactical levels when considering the purchase or design of an online assessment data management system. We discuss the usage of e-portfolios for storing and reviewing student work in the creative disciplines, and provide sources for further information concerning the assessment of student learning online.

Online Assessment: Where to Begin

As we specified in the chapter on assessment models, our overall standpoint is that theory-based and model-based assessment is even more a necessity for online programs than purely traditional on-ground programs. First, the advent of online learning offers the possibility of collecting large amounts of data about our students' learning, their background characteristics, and their interactions. A theory- and model-based approach to assessment in online programs will help clarify what is most essential to know about our students' performance; without such guidance it is not uncommon to see data fishing expeditions develop rather than focused assessment schemas. Second, a theory or model based approach affords the distinct advantage of keeping what we need to assess in the foreground despite the incessant and rapid change in technology, thus permitting easier adaptation to new systems and advances in technology.

For faculty charged with understanding, assessing, and improving student learning in creative disciplines, the online environment offers some distinct advantages regarding the kind and quality of information that can be collected not only on individual student learning, but also on groups of students. Though assessment is often seen more as an unwelcome intrusion and imposition, we've happily discovered that it has framed a series of useful and challenging college-wide discussions about what we do.

For example, in the online environment we can easily collect information on learner characteristics and background, the demonstration of student competencies relative to faculty expectations for learning, student gains in metacognitive abilities through reflective writing in e-portfolios, student satisfaction, the faculty experience, faculty-student interaction and feedback, student-student interaction, student interaction with the virtual interface and elements of the learning management system (Moore, 1989), comparative performance, progress, and retention of our students, and program outcomes such as professional placement and further professional education. In this context, Davies (2010) offers a good summary of reasons for taking assessment online:

- Greater variety and authenticity in assessment designs
- Improved learner engagement, for example through interactive formative assessments with adaptive feedback
- Choice in the timing and location of assessments
- Capture of wider skills and attributes not easily assessed by other means, for example through simulations, e-portfolios, and interactive games
- Efficient submission, marking [grading], moderation and data storage processes

- Consistent, accurate results with opportunities to combine human and computer marking [grading]
- Immediate feedback
- Increased opportunities for learners to act on feedback, for example by reflection in e-portfolios
- Innovative approaches based around use of creative media and online peer and self-assessment
- Accurate, timely and accessible evidence on the effectiveness of curriculum design and delivery (p. 8-9)

Faculty members teaching in online programs utilize a broad array of learning activities, with attendant broad implications for e-Assessment. Students in digital media programs create works in electronic format as a matter of course. Students are highly accustomed to using social media, and a number of learning activities in the online environment are reflective of our general move towards socially constructed knowledge. Overall, the goal should be to use learning activities for assessment that allow students to demonstrate their competence in a variety of ways that move them towards professional practice (cf. Giloi and du Toit, 2013), and ideally to triangulate our assessments as previously discussed in the chapter on technical foundations. For example, learning activities might include asynchronous or synchronous (real-time) online discussion forums, collaborative creation of art and design products and artifacts (for example through blogs or through collaborative content management systems such as Microsoft SharePoint), online journaling and reflective self-assessments, and student e-portfolios at the course and/or degree program level. Adaptive learning tools, hitherto used primarily to assess and guide student learning in disciplines such as mathematics and sciences, can also be adapted to creative disciplines, for example to aid students' systematic acquisition of model-based reasoning in design thinking. Excellent resources are available that provide specific strategies for integrating assessment practice into online courses and curricula, for example Palloff and Pratt (2008). Crisp (2011) also offers a relevant and readable overview on e-Assessment for faculty at http://www.transformingassessment.com/moodle/file.php/84/Handbook_for_teachers.pdf.

The shift to online program offerings also affects the array of assessment tools available. To assess student work and the signs and traces of student learning in the online environment, not only will we continue to utilize direct and indirect methods, but the role of passive assessment will become much more prevalent—among other reasons, because it is unobtrusive, saves both time and labor, and results in rich data across our students. One of the largest portals currently available for e-assessment tools is through www.transformingassessment.com, where "Examples of technologies showcased in the context of e-assessment include, discussion forums, voice boards, virtual classroom platforms, social networking (Facebook, Twitter, Linkedin), multimedia (YouTube, Flickr, QVR), e-portfolios, blogs, wikis, serious games, simulations, virtual worlds (second life, open sim, thinking worlds), voting/polling (votapedia, clickers), L.M.S (Moodle, Blackboard/Webct), virtual labs, remote labs and augmented reality." (Crisp and Hillier, n.d.).

Direct assessment will continue to be the tool of choice for most assessment of student work. Most of the major online assessment management systems and e-portfolio systems incorporate the ability to view student work online, develop and utilize an embedded rubric to rate the student work, the ability to generate comments back to the student, and the ability to store both the ratings of student competence and faculty-provided commentary. Student inventories and diagnostic instruments can be administered within most learning management systems. Indirect assessment methods including surveys can be administered within the learning management system or sent directly to student email accounts. Text-based asynchronous (or synchronous) online focus groups can be used to explore student perceptions around an area of interest, to better gauge how students are thinking about a phenomenon of interest.

Unobtrusive or passive assessment assumes major importance in the online environment. The basic notion is to embed unobtrusive assessment measures and utilize the online environment for signs and artifacts of student learning and expression (Gibson and Webb, 2013). Schute (2011) refers to this form of assessment as 'stealth' assessment, since it is seamless to the learner. Passive assessment might include online competency-based assessment, content analysis of students reviewing and discussing each other's designs and models, textual data from online discussion and interaction threads, and unobtrusive observation of student choices in a simulation, among many other possibilities (Gibson and Webb, 2013). Combined with background information on student characteristics such as demographics, educational goals and motivations, and learning style preferences, unobtrusive/passive assessment methods may help faculty at the course and program level to form a highly cohesive picture of student learning, information that can be used in a formative context to effect continual adjustments to pedagogy and to furthering student learning.

Challenges of Implementing Online Assessment Data Management Systems

Why should we take assessment data management online? Machiavelli noted that nothing is as risky or unsure of the outcome as introducing a new order of things...so why introduce change? Introducing an online assessment data management system across the university or college is a special case of organizational development – a system-wide intervention – and one that can achieve tangible benefits in terms of time and labor savings, leveraging everyone's effort to maximize results, providing a viable structure for the sharing of assessment information and good practices across a program, department, or college (Hoey, 2008). But it is important to note that technology-based solutions for assessment are not a silver bullet by themselves. A vital distinction to make is that between *conducting* assessment of student activities online and *tracking* assessment online (Rogers, 2010). The former includes the faculty-driven processes of defining appropriate student learning outcomes, developing an appropriate schema for program-level assessment, selecting assessment tools, and actually assessing student artifacts, typically via the grading process. The latter involves the collection, analysis, reflection, and reporting of assessment results. Both are important yet discrete activities.

The sheer number of students in a studio or course, courses in a program, and programs in a college or university frequently makes using technology solutions to assessment, institutional effectiveness. and accreditation a necessity. However, a very real problem for those who contemplate the introduction of assessment data management systems is the opposite of the 1989 film *Field of Dreams*: Just because we build it does *not* mean they'll come! Oakleaf et al. (2013) note that the "Adoption of an AMS [Assessment Management System] by faculty and librarians is not assured" (p.101) for reasons including perceptions of no distinct advantage over previous practice, perceived incompatibility with faculty work, lack of visibility on campus, and inability to give the system a trial run before using it.

Adopting online systems for assessment data management forces decisions and change: we should be aware of that and plan for it. Knowing the organizational culture and politics before introducing a systemic change is crucial—since we can never change just one thing in an organization without affecting other areas. Broad representation across campus is essential in planning for the introduction of an online assessment management system, and as RiCharde (2009) points out, representation should absolutely include information technology staff to serve as general advisors and to ensure that technical glitches are avoided in implementation. The task at hand is to make online assessment and data management easy, user-friendly, culturally viable, and overwhelmingly beneficial to teaching and learning. The goal of the intervention is to make it easy for faculty to engage in conversations about what students are learning based on data, not anecdote. It's a tool to facilitate evidence-based discussion, reflection, planning, and ongoing adjustments.

Organizational culture is one of the most resilient characteristics of developed organizations (Schein, 1991). For us, this is a bedrock concept to understand before we begin constructing or implementing an online assessment data management system. Culture concerns the values and beliefs we hold about the organization's purpose, role, and reason for existence. It's about the behavioral norms to which we adhere, and roles that we take in that organization to accomplish what we collectively believe the organizational purposes. Tolan and Hurney (2004) address the underlying cultural barriers to the integration of assessment in plain terms: "The 'elephant' on the table' that no one wants to talk about is the decisions and systems change that must accompany implementation, and the deep cultural change that must occur in the organization to sustain outcomes assessment."

Adding to the complexity of change implementation is the existence of multiple cultures within our institutions. Bergquist and Pawlak (2007) define six distinct cultures in higher education (collegial, managerial, developmental, advocacy, virtual, and tangible) and demonstrate how the image, historical traditions, and character of institutions are shaped by the six cultures interacting within them. To the larger notion of institutional culture we need to add the differences in disciplinary culture, especially among creative disciplines. In moving creative programs and assessment of those programs online, our task is one of managing the translations of meaning among the cultures. The conflict between virtual learning and traditional classroom-based faculty cultures, in particular, has been the basis of much conflict; especially prior to the advent of

MOOCs and the cultural legitimation that format has brought to online teaching and learning. At the end of the day, only a culturally sensitive and politically informed effort will stand a reasonable chance of achieving the desired outcomes of sustainable assessment, and institutional effectiveness in complex institutional environments.

Another challenge to implementing online assessment data management systems involves the very real question of power distribution and the impact of power differentials on trust. Evaluation and assessment are in fact political processes in which some people have more power than others (Palumbo, 1987). Knowing that, we much choose our steps carefully.Taking data from the confines of the classroom to the program level represents a huge power shift in higher education, one that presupposes the development of a high degree of trust. Success demands that we develop a politically astute implementation plan with support and articulated expectations from the faculty senate, committees, deans, provost, president, and other persons of influence. In practice, successful change managers will observe, map and utilize extant coalitions, social networks, and both formal and informal power relationships in the institution to ensure successful implementation and sustainability of online assessment systems (Boone et al., 2002).

Common Online Assessment Management Systems

The single most comprehensive listing of tools to help manage assessment processes and assessment data is found at http://www2.acs.ncsu.edu/ UPA/archives/assmt/resource.htm, the Internet Resources for Higher Education Assessment portal, under the section heading 'tools to help organize assessment information.' Hoey (2008) provides background on the derivation and types of online assessment management systems: First is a group of systems of which several are commercially available and widely used, but have their origins as a single-institution solution, usually to prepare for an accreditation visit. This group includes Mentor by Axiom (Fairfield University); WEAVE Online (Virginia Commonwealth University); PRISM/PEARL (Colorado State University) OATS (Georgia Tech), and a number of others. The second group was developed by vendors who have responded to the need to prepare for specialized accreditation requirements, especially teacher education. These systems usually feature an ability to disaggregate assessment and student data down to the level of the individual student, as NCATE requires. Representative systems include TracDat, e-Lumen, LiveText, TaskStream, and Tk20. A third group of online assessment data management systems was developed by those vendors who had already developed learning management systems, such as Blackboard (Blackboard Learn). These systems are designed to integrate with the learning management solutions developed by the same vendor. Regardless of the origins of the system, a rigorous, inclusive, and structured decision process will best serve an institution as it prepares for development or purchase and implementation.

Deciding on Most Important and Viable Features: What Criteria Should We Use?

Once a collaborative decision has been made to move ahead with initial piloting or full implementation of an online assessment management system, it is important not to put the cart before the horse and adopt the first system at hand. Our colleagues will benefit from our first identifying structured decision criteria and features we'd like to see in an online assessment data management system, and following through on a rigorous comparison. We should ask both what is most important and what is most viable given the decision criteria (Hoey, 2008; RiCharde, 2009; Oakleaf et al., 2013). Our decision criteria might include:

- Likelihood of widespread and sustained use by faculty, staff, and administrators
- Ease of use, by even the least technologically adept philistine
- Cost
- Technical support needs, and technical support available from the vendor
- Development time needed prior to roll-out
- Proven success of the system at other creative institutions
- Examples of the feature sets that are important to consider
- Extent to which system supports regional and specialized accreditation
- Types and amount of data that can be included, and level at which disaggregation is possible
- Annual roll-over and archiving of data, so nothing is lost and longitudinal comparisons may be made
- Ability of the product to integrate with student and/or other databases or systems

Questions to Consider: Strategic, Tactical, and Logistical

Expanding on the set of basic decision criteria above, this section provides questions that may serve as a guide to the strategic, tactical, and operational/logistical questions to consider when developing or purchasing an online data management system. First, at the strategic level, we should ask ourselves:

- What decisions do we aim to put in place and what should we therefore measure?
- What level of assessment are we dealing with, and therefore what level of detail do we expect to see? Individual assignments? Student-level? Course-level? Program or college level? A rule of thumb is to start at the most granular level – for example, the individual assignment level within a course.
- Are we to integrate this application with others for reporting, planning, proposal-writing, or other purposes?
- To what extent should the system:
    - Map to institutional strategic plan and goals?

- Map to institutional budgeting and resource allocation processes?
- Map to specialized and regional accreditation criteria for assessment and educational effectiveness?
- Interact directly with an online compliance system for specialized and regional accreditation?

Having addressed strategic questions concerning a proposed assessment system, tactical questions are next: The basic operational question is 'what do we want the system to do?' Should it:

- Map assessment data to student learning outcomes? At what level – individual assignment, course-level, student e-portfolio, program-level, and institutional?
- Integrate with an online LMS/CMS such as Blackboard or eCollege, and map to individual courses taught in the institution each term?
- Facilitate assessment data collection online? If so, what kinds of data?
  - Enable faculty to conduct and record individual student assessments?
  - Facilitate recording of program-level assessment of student work by groups of faculty?
  - Data from online assessment of student projects?
  - Data from online exams?
  - Electronic portfolio information?
  - Evidence of student metacognitive development as an artist through reflective writing?
- Act as an assessment data repository? If so, for what data, at what level, and for what period of time? Should it include:
  - Jury results? Licensure test results?
  - Standardized tests?
  - Supervisor evaluations of co-op or internship experiences?
  - Course-level assignments and student work?
  - Midpoint and senior design project data from programs?
  - Student course evaluations?
- Track use of assessment information to spur changes in curricula over time?
- Permit aggregation and analysis of roll-up trend data over time for program review?
- Facilitate assessment of non-academic, co-curricular and support service units?
- Track assessment plans and results?
- Permit summarization of assessment data?
- Permit easy analysis of assessment data?
- Permit analysis of similar outcomes across various programs for general education?
- Link assessment data with other institutional data sources?
  - Demographic and student performance information from student databases?

- Keep all data sources synchronized to avoid multiple data re-entry, to minimize source data variance and avoid the "my numbers are right, your numbers are wrong" syndrome?

Having sorted out what we expect an online assessment management system to be able to do, the next set of questions to be considered encompasses logistical considerations: How should the system work and even more explicitly, who is going to do the work? The set of issues detailed below all deserve consideration.

- Data entry and maintenance process
  - how will data be entered into the system?
  - how will data be organized within the system?
  - how may data and information be viewed from within the system?
  - who will maintain the data and the system?
- Annual or periodic data collection and update process
  - who will collect the data?
  - who will enter the data? Will it be done seamlessly as part of the grading process for assignments and projects?
  - who will organize the data and analyze it?
  - who will report the results?
  - who will discuss the data and develop an action plan around the results?
- Software issues
  - From whence should the system be accessible?
- Database issues
  - Will the system be compatible with various operating systems on campus and online?
  - Will the system be compatible with various databases on campus and online?
- Security issues
  - Who should have access, and at what level?
  - How important is transparency of all information?
  - To what information should there be access?

RiCharde (2009) and Oakleaf et al. (2013) provide further resources on selection criteria and desirable feature sets in online assessment data management systems; the latter resource includes an explicit feature-by-feature comparison of some of the more popular systems. Also worth noting is that the same points concerning roll-out planning as described in the chapter on achieving assessment success also apply to planning the implementation of an online assessment data management system – perhaps to an even higher degree.

Summary for Online Assessment Management Systems

To summarize this section of the chapter, moving to an online assessment data management system surfaces multiple organizational issues. The changes needed may not necessarily mesh with norms of organizational culture and politics, so we are well advised to begin with a solid understanding of those aspects of college and university life. When evaluating various alternatives and vendors, using a clear set of criteria and focused questions at the strategic, operational, and tactical level can facilitate a more rigorous and comparative decision that will serve the institution well. Beginning our roll-out planning early is another key to success.

E-Portfolios

Electronic portfolios, or e-portfolios are covered extensively in book-length works by numerous authors (Light et al, 2011; Cambridge, 2010; van Nood, 2013; Wills & Rice, 2013; Buzzetto-More, 2010; Wankel & Blessinger, 2012). Here we will provide an overview and suggest further resources, as e-portfolios are one tool where students can collect their work and where assessment opportunities can be richly mined. Courses and programs use e-portfolios for many different reasons. "Electronic portfolios are designed for organizing, sharing, and presenting work done in the program; for reflecting on experiences, both in the program and during field/internship experiences; for sharing personal beliefs, goals, and ongoing professional growth. In addition to the student's experience, colleges often use the portfolio for assessment activities. Whether for accreditation or for program improvement, the portfolio can also serve as an important source of data to drive program changes." ("Effective e-Portfolios", 2011, p. 4).

E-portfolios can be generally divided into three main categories or types of portfolios: professional, program, and reflective. Professional are focused on the individual's experiences and are created in order to gain employment or to track professional development. "Program portfolios are a way for the program to collect critical assignments that are used to track the student's growth while in the program" ("Effective e-Portfolios", p. 4). "Reflective portfolios are usually structured around program goals or outcomes and are focused on collecting activities and journals from the student in which they present and describe how they have worked toward and achieved these goals" ("Effective e-Portfolios", p. 4).

E-portfolios become effective assessment tools when they contain required elements (sometimes referred to as "key artifacts") for the course and/or program plus student self-selected artifacts (Dawn, et al, 2011). Some benefits of an e-portfolio are as follows:

- All artifacts including documents, images, and multimedia files can be uploaded to one secure online location, which acts like an external hard-drive to protect files from computer crashes, loss, or theft.
- Because of the nature of electronic portfolios, they lend themselves to all three types of assessment methods: direct, indirect, and passive.
- Students can use their e-portfolio while they are in school, to help obtain a job during and/or after their educations, and on into their professional careers for advancement and job changes.
- Embedded assessment features in some e-portfolio systems make it easier to manage quantitative and qualitative data (Dawn et al, 2011).

While the benefits of using an e-portfolio for both student work and for assessment activities in the course, program, and school-wide levels are numerous, the primary challenge in using the systems lies in training for students, faculty, and staff. The goal of using any system should be "to get away from faculty compliance, but to create a rich process that becomes an integral part of how a program operates" (OTIS Assessment Tools). Many learning management and assessment systems have been installed, tried, and then abandoned due to not enough widespread training and implementing of what the systems are actually capable of doing, and this becomes frustrating for everyone on campus involved in using the system. The other challenge is the expense to the institution and sometimes to the students using the system. As said previously in this chapter numerous e-portfolio systems are available through commercial vendors. As with assessment data management systems, some were originally developed as in-house assessment solutions. One example is Digication (developed at RISD), examples of which may be seen at https://risd.digication.com/portfolio/directory.digi?sid=2&cid=0&tid=0&pid=8677&. Two websites are excellent references on e-Portfolio systems. The first is available at http://www2.acs.ncsu.edu/UPA/archives/assmt/resource.htm, the Internet Resources for Higher Education Outcomes Assessment website, and the second is website of AABEEL, The Association for Authentic, Experiential, and Evidence-Based Learning, "a professional association for the world ePortfolio community."

Other Online Assessment Tools for Institutional Processes

The earlier chapter on Dimensions and Continua of Assessment explicates a table of what assessment tools might be useful at various points in the student life cycle. One of those points is for information obtained prior to matriculation. Assessment of student applicants is a very basic and time-intensive process for faculty and for admissions officers, not to mention for students. Traditionally, the information from entrance exams and auditions is hardly used past the admissions process, even though it could be used as a baseline assessment for the value-added gains in learning and professionalism of individual and entering groups of students, at both the undergraduate and graduate levels. For instance, one of the authors of this book sat for music history, music theory, 16th and 18th counterpoint, and several other demanding entrance exams as an incoming graduate student at a large school of music in the southern United States. Apart from the use of those exams as a placement device, no further use was made of the data as a baseline to evaluate and demonstrate to outsiders the value of the music programs. This represents a missed opportunity!

Fortunately, at least one product is now available that facilitates the collection of portfolios, audition recordings, and other critical information on applicants, and that could be used to archive relevant audition and entrance exams. Decision Desk (http://www.decisiondesk.com/) is described as an applicant tracking system and management software—the first of a new breed of applications that, like assessment data management systems, leverage the power of information technology to simplify and facilitate candidate applications as well as admissions decisions based on faculty assessment of student work and/or performance. Of interest for those in creative disciplines, the software includes specific modules for visual arts and performing arts.

Further Resources on e-Assessment

A number of associations and further resources on e-Assessment have developed as online education has grown. As listed in www.transformingassessment.com, these resources comprise associations, newsletters, conferences, and other portals.

> eAA - eAssessment Association. According to their website, "The eAA has 3 major goals: - to provide professional support for workers in this field of expertise; create and communicate the positive contributions that technology makes to assessment and produce a statement of good practice for commercial organisations." They are based in the UK and has been active since 2008. http://www.e-assessment.com/

> International Journal of e-Assessment is the web home for journal articles on e-Assessment. Users must register to access the site but registration is free. http://journals.sfu.ca/ijea/index.php/journal/login?source=%2Fijea%2Findex.php%2Fjournal%2Fannouncement

> JISC - Technology-enhanced assessment is a UK-based organization that offers programs, publishes research, and provides an electronic home for all things related to technology-enhanced assessment. http://www.jisc.ac.uk/whatwedo/programmes/elearning/assessment.asp

> SQA - Scottish Qualifications Authority The SQA website is devoted to e-assessment, and features case studies, information on e-portfolios, and other resources for learners, employers, teachers or lecturers, and others associated with education. http://www.sqa.org.uk/sqa/5607.html

> Assessment Tomorrow Ltd has run a website since its 2003 inception that "provides comprehensive and innovative e-Assessment management, advice, support, and project management to Education and Training from the class-room to the workplace." http://www.assessmenttomorrow.com/

> International Computer Assisted Assessment (CAA) Conference happens annually in the UK with tracks on assessing students skills and enhancing student learning, evaluation, reporting, strategic developments, and innovations in computer assisted assessments. http://caaconference.co.uk/

References

Bergquist, W. and Pawlak, K. (2007). *Engaging the Six Cultures of the Academy*. San Francisco: Jossey-Bass.

Boone, E., Jones, J. and Safrit, R. (2002). *Developing Programs in Adult Education: A Conceptual Programming Model* (2nd Edition). Long Grove, IL: Waveland Press, Inc.

Buzetto-More, N. (2010). *The E-Portfolio Paradigm: Informing, Educating, and Managing with E-Portfolios.* Santa Rosa, CA: Informing Science Press.

Cambridge, D. (2010). *E-Portfolios for Lifelong Learning and Assessment.* San Francisco: Jossey-Bass.

Crisp, G. and Hillier, M. (n.d.). Transforming Assessment. Retrieved from http://www.transformingassessment.com/fellowship.php.

Crisp, G. (2011). *Teacher's Handbook on e-Assessment*. Retrieved from http://www.transformingassessment.com/moodle/file.php/84/Handbook_for_teachers.pdf.

Davies, S. (2010). Effective Assessment in a Digital Age: A guide to technology-enhanced assessment and feedback. Retrieved from http://www.jisc.ac.uk/media/documents/programmes/elearning/digiassass_eada.pdf

Dawn, S. et al. (2011). Electronic portfolios: questions, implementation, and lessons learned in a doctor of pharmacy program. *Currents in Pharmacy Teaching and Learning.* 3(2011), 164-170.

Effective e-Portfolios: 2011 Training Guides. (2011) LiveText. LaGrange, IL.

Giloi, S. and du Toit, P. (2013). Current Approaches to the Assessment of Graphic Design in a Higher Education Context. *International Journal of Art and Design Education*, 32(2), 256-268.

Hoey, J. (2008). The Politics and Practicalities of Online Assessment Data Management Systems. Presentation at the Association for Institutional Research Annual Forum, Seattle, WA.

Light, T.P., Chen, H.L., & Ittelson, J.C. (2011). *Documenting Learning with ePortfolios: a guide for college instructors.* San Francisco: Jossey-Bass.

Oakleaf, M., Belanger, J., & Graham, C. (2013). Choosing and Using Assessment Management Systems: What Librarians Need to Know. Paper presented at ACRL 2013, Indianapolis, IN.

Otis Assessment Tools for Smart and/or Attractive People. Retrieved from http://otis.coe.uky.edu/portfolio.php.

Palloff, R. and Pratt, K. (2008). *Assessing the Online Learner: Resources and Strategies for Faculty*. San Francisco: Jossey-Bass.

Palumbo, D., Editor (1987). *The Politics of Program Evaluation*. Beverly Hills, CA: Sage Publications.

RiCharde, R. S. (2009). Data Management and Data Management Tools. In Peat, B., and Moriarty, L. (Eds.), *Assessing Criminal Justice/Criminology Education: A Resource Handbook for Educators and Administrators.* Chapel Hill: University of North Carolina Press.

Rogers, G. (2010, July 28th). Program Assessment of Student Learning blog, Retrieved from http://programassessment.blogspot.com/2010_07_01_archive.html.

Schein, E. (1991). *Organizational Culture and Leadership*. San Francisco: Jossey-Bass.

Tolan, L..A., and Hurny, J.J. (2004, June). Resources, organizational change and data systems: Issues and problems in the implementation of outcomes assessment. *Proceedings from 2004 American Society for EngineeringEducation Annual Conference and Exposition*, Salt Lake City.

van Nood, R. (2013). *The Power of E-Portfolios: Document, Reflect, & Share Learning with Evernote.* Seattle, WA: Amazon Digital Services.

Wankel, L.A. & Blessinger, P. (2012) *Increasing Student Engagement and Retention Using Social Technologies: Facebook, E-Portfolios, and Other Social Networking Technologies.* Bingley, U.K.: Emerald Publishing Group.

Wills, K. & Rice, R. (2013). *ePortfolio Performance Support Systems: Constructing, Presenting, and Assessing Portfolios.* Anderson, S.C.: Parlor Press.

Chapter 9: Achieving Assessment Success

"At first people refuse to believe that a strange new thing can be done, then they begin to hope it can be done, then they see it can be done – then it is done and all the world wonders why it was not done centuries ago."
— F. H. Burnett (1911), *The Secret Garden*

Having a roadmap and a set of guideposts is important in any journey, and the process of putting together an assessment system in the creative disciplines is no exception. This chapter integrates and brings together the themes we have discussed in earlier chapters. The chapter includes a discussion of change management, sources of resistance to beginning a program of assessment, and other likely bumps in the road. The organic and gradual development of a sustainable assessment program, from the individual student to the program, college, and institution level is detailed. The chapter concludes by providing direction in the development of a sustainable assessment program and characteristics of what a "developed" assessment system might look like in the creative and performing arts.

Faculty Involvement in Assessment

Earlier in this volume, we reflected on how assessment was introduced as a top-down initiative in much of American higher education, the consequences of which have been high resistance and only a slow embrace of the concepts underlying assessment. However, substantial progress has taken place over the last twenty-five years (Hutchings, 2010). The scholarship of assessment, teaching, and learning has advanced tremendously, and in many ways it is now to the advantage of the creative disciplines to engage with assessment, since a well-developed literature exists, a solid body of good practice has emerged. Furthermore, the undertaking of assessment has been made substantially easier through the innovative use of information technology (Ewell, 2010), an area we discuss in more detail in the chapter on online assessment.

Hutchings (2010) elaborates a number of barriers that have hitherto discouraged faculty involvement in assessment, including the use of an unfamiliar vocabulary, the perception that assessment is only about external accountability and standardized testing, a lack of training in assessment, the lack of congruence between college and university reward systems and the work of assessment, and in many instances the lack of sufficient and convincing evidence that assessment makes a positive difference. To that set of barriers, we might add the long tradition of continuous, informal feedback and individual mentoring within the atelier, unlike many liberal arts and professional disciplines. How are these barriers to be overcome in creative disciplines? With the twin objectives of increasing both the likelihood of faculty involvement and the quality of assessment, Hutchings (2010) proposes six ways to align the work of faculty and the purposes of assessment:

1. Build assessment around the regular, ongoing work of teaching and learning;
2. Make a place for assessment in faculty development;
3. Integrate assessment into the preparation of graduate students;
4. Reframe assessment as scholarship;
5. Create campus spaces and occasions for constructive assessment conversation and action; and
6. Involve students in assessment (p.3).

The wide needs for higher education faculty involvement in assessment at the graduate level and in preparing the future professoriate have also been recognized nationally. Recommendations to increase the involvement in assessment among current faculty from the Council of Graduate Schools' (2011) report, *Preparing Future Faculty to Assess Student Learning*, include:

- Promoting the recognition that assessment is a faculty governance issue, i.e., through faculty governance boards or other forums;
- Facilitating faculty access to assessment tools, which can make the process of assessment more transparent;
- Giving faculty members opportunities to share their own effective assessment strategies and experiences with other faculty members (Denecke et al., 2011, p.39).

Established faculty organizations in the United States have added their collective voice to the dialogue about faculty involvement in assessment. Gold et al. (2011) note that three national faculty unions, including the American Association of University Professors (AAUP), the American Federation of Teachers (AFT), and the National Education Association (NEA) affirm the centrality of the faculty role in how assessment should be done and how results should be used, agreeing that "faculty involvement in assessment is essential in order to insure that the principles of academic freedom and shared governance are honored in all phases of the assessment process" (Gold et al., 2011, p.3).

While the importance of faculty involvement in assessment is widespread, the recognition of the need by itself is not sufficient for progress to be made. Careful planning, an awareness of cultures within creative disciplines, purposefully building a healthy faculty dialogue, having an understanding of how change proceeds within the college and university context, making expert resources about assessment available, and perhaps above all communicating clearly, ideally leveraging social media, are all important facets of implementing assessment in creative disciplines and institutions. Starting from scratch, how might that proceed in an organic manner?

Organic Evolution of Assessment—From Individual to Institutional Levels of Inquiry

In developing a sustainable approach to assessment, the first steps are often the most difficult. Creating ongoing faculty dialogue on assessment issues, especially evidence-based dialogue, is the highest priority. Understanding the vocabulary and worldview of the disciplines is vital to promulgating clear communication in a style and manner that is more likely to be understood. For example, faculty in Architecture and in Music may not have a similar disciplinary ethos or communicate in the same manner, yet translating structural concepts from the architectonics of music to the envelope of a building may offer a way to establish common understanding. As first step in establishing faculty communication and dialogue around assessment, Hoey (1995) reports on using university-wide faculty focus groups at North Carolina State University as one way of doing this. Whatever process is used, beginning a dialogue among faculty is a vital first step forward.

As we alluded to earlier, at the outset it is important to keep in mind that multiple loci for assessment exist in most institutions:

- Individual student assessment, for which we will need individualized student learning outcomes;
- Assessment of multiple students at the course or studio level, for which we need course-level or studio-level student learning outcomes;
- Program-level assessment, requiring program-level student learning outcomes, and finally
- Assessment at the institutional level, requiring institution-level student learning outcomes – usually stated broadly, at a high level of abstraction.

Assessment of student learning outcomes happens in creative disciplines as a matter of course between faculty and individual students, yielding granular information that faculty use to understand a student's current state of artistic development and needed further direction. Faculty in creative disciplines have used such assessment informally for hundreds of years – but what has not happened to the same degree is the purposeful assembly and analysis of assessment information across multiple students, discussions around the implications for student learning, and adjustments to teaching and curriculum to improve student learning – in other words, effectively 'closing the loop' (Ballard, 2013). When collected assessment information becomes a shared object of discussion among faculty, conversations eventually turn to the need for looking at students' learning more broadly than the studio experience and individual courses. At that point, programs and departments begin to evolve towards a consideration of the entire curriculum. Are there 'gateway' courses where substantial numbers of students experience difficulty term after term? How many and what percentage of our students fail color theory the first time through, and why? Do our music students have a broad knowledge of the music business, and how do we know? What are faculty and relevant external stakeholders seeing or not seeing in capstone projects, designs, and performances? Posing such questions in turn leads to a re-examination of how faculty have stated program-level expectations for student learning in the form of learning outcomes, and usually leads to further sharpening and focusing of how those student learning outcomes are articulated.

When conversations evolve to the point of addressing an entire program of study, colleagues naturally want to be able to have information that can be used to discern opportunities for making adjustments across the curriculum, and at that point a more systematic approach to assessment becomes valuable and informative, using tools such as curriculum maps and collectively designed and calibrated rubrics. Once such information begins to be available to faculty, it has been our experience that conversations deepen, requests for better and more focused assessment information surface, and a process of purposeful, systematic curriculum adjustment and renewal takes root at the department or program level, grounded in the student learning outcomes faculty have identified. But it does not stop there.

Two facts of college and university life are that we speak with our colleagues and that we have a faculty governance system, one in which faculty participate in a number of committees. Conversations about student learning are a natural fit for curriculum committees and general education committees, for example, and provide a forum for the diffusion of findings from assessment studies undertaken in one or more departments. The desire to understand how and where students are gaining oral and written communication skills, an understanding of ethics, critical and reflective thinking abilities, mathematical and spatial relations skills, the ability to work in interdisciplinary teams on projects, and other important student learning outcomes may precipitate reflection on how a program of general education is structured across the institution. From that point, the same faculty desire to understand how and what students learn that prompted the development of a systematized approach at the department or program level may prompt a collective inquiry into the nature of a college education across the institution, what students should be expected to learn, and the informational bases/assessments that will be used to understand the extent to which students are in fact developing and demonstrating the knowledge, skills, and abilities faculty expect of someone to be awarded a degree or diploma. Many institutions have developed institutional or educational effectiveness committees for precisely this reason.

The Development of Systematic Approaches to Institutional Effectiveness

Once we begin to examine assessment evidence and gain a systematic understanding of our needs for course and curricular adjustment and change at the program, school, and institution level, the question of resources comes into play—but increasingly from an evidence-based standpoint, to support improvements in student learning—rather than a primarily political and reputational perspective. Does the evidence from senior capstone projects point to our students needing more experiential learning opportunities, such as internships, co-ops, or undergraduate research? If so, what does the evidence base indicate would be most effective, and what is the cost of such an undertaking in terms of faculty time, advisors, outreach to the creative and design community and industries? Undertaking an inquiry on these questions, making recommendations, and ultimately pursuing a course of action would be difficult and tenuous without a supportive institutional infrastructure. Fortunately, such infrastructure generally already exists, and we can integrate assessment with those processes to ensure its sustainability within the institution.

Department, college, and university annual planning retreats and reporting processes; periodic academic program reviews; and strategic planning processes, as basic elements of institutional infrastructure and functioning, have traditionally concentrated on the inputs and reputational factors of higher education, yet these same processes can be repositioned and redesigned to serve evidence-based improvements in student learning (Hoey and Bosworth, 2009). For example, Bresciani (2006) describes a process for redeveloping academic program review around reflective inquiry on student learning; Middaugh (2009) provides practical advice for alignment of institutional planning and goal-setting, assessment, analysis, reporting, and resource allocation processes that utilize information derived through assessment, not only within academics but across the college or university to maximize the ability of the institution to meet its educational mission. Taking assessment and the ongoing use of assessment information to such a systems standpoint across an entire institution is usually referred to as institutional effectiveness. Many institutions have developed their own guides or handbooks to assist faculty, departments, and administrative units with implementing an evidence-based approach to institutional effectiveness (e.g., Texas A&M International University, 2010).

As pointed out in the chapter on Dimensions and Continua of Assessment, regional, national, and many specialized accreditation agency criteria have been fundamentally repositioned over the past 25 years to emphasize student learning and the outcomes of education rather than size of the library holdings, the endowment, or the physical plant. At the regional and national level, these criteria effectively mandate the development of formative assessment systems and institutional effectiveness within our programs, schools, and institutions. Similarities across the regional accreditors with regard to assessment expectations have been well-summarized by Provezis (2010).

Support and Resources Needed for Assessment to Flourish

We have discussed how assessment implementation might grow from the individual to the institutional level as an organic, faculty-driven endeavor. Readers will have identified from their own experiences that pervasive support for assessment must also be provided at each stage and at each level for it to take root and be sustained. In this section, we provide several recommendations. Palomba and Banta (1999), Suskie (2009), Walvoord (2010) and other standard reference works on assessment provide further insights.

Having informed resources available to faculty is perhaps the most basic need. We cannot expect someone to do a completely new and seemingly strange task without a lot of guidance and on-demand expert consultation. Sufficient availability of consultative, one-on-one assessment planning and support is critical. We have to be able to provide cogent advice on questions like: How can this be done and still meet teaching, creative activity, and service demands? How can it work for me?

Resources that should ideally be made available for faculty include assessment subject matter experts to act in a consultative role, web-based informational resources, and suitable professional development opportunities including conference attendance, support through assessment mini-grants, on-campus or online training opportunities, and one or more campus (or online) forums for dialogue on assessment issues. The overall goal should be to provide pervasive support. Some institutions provide professional assessment support for faculty through a teaching and learning center. Vanderbilt University, for example, offers a certificate program in teaching that includes intensive exposure to assessment practices, see http://cft.vanderbilt.edu/programs/certificate-in-college-teaching/. Among creative institutions, Otis College of Art and Design offers a rich set of assessment resources to faculty on its institutional effectiveness and assessment website at http://www.otis.edu/institutional-effectiveness-assessment. Faculty or staff acting as an assessment resources need to be familiar with their own and other creative disciplines, how faculty in the institution have already been undertaking assessment, methods of data collection and analysis, use of technology for assessment, instrument construction, the appropriate use of rubrics and other assessment methods. Ideally, those acting as assessment resources should also possess well-honed communication skills and an ample measure of emotional intelligence.

To summarize this section: Three principles of change management are relevant to the design and implementation of assessment systems. First, an awareness and perception of need for change in how things are done must be present, and our goal should be to create sufficient dialogue for that felt need to emerge (Boone et al., 2002). Second, we should leverage extant organizational opportunities and synergies for change wherever and whenever possible (Ewell, 1984). Third, the extent to which we make it easier for faculty to adopt a new way of doing things than staying with the old way, the diffusion of the change will be facilitated—and to paraphrase F.H. Burnett (1911), everyone will wonder why systematic assessment of student learning outcomes was not introduced years ago.

Roadmap to Success

Following a planned change outline, this part of the chapter provides a roadmap for putting together an assessment effort at the department, college, and institutional level. The exact order, timing, emphasis, and inclusion of elements in the roadmap will vary across institutions, but successful implementations of assessment systems tend to include the following processsual tasks (Hoey and Bosworth, 2009; Boone et al., 2002).

- *Secure the support of top leadership.* Nothing happens without it.

- *Inventory what already exists.* Develop an inventory of the assessment methods currently in use. Methods usually exist, but not in an organized format where communication of good practices may be facilitated. Ballard (2013) recounts such an inventory process at Otis College of Art and Design.
- *Develop a master intervention planning framework* for the planning, needs definition, implementation, evaluation, and follow-up phases of assessment implementation. As a conceptual framework, use a collaborative planned change model such as Boone et al. (2002) for guidance. Plan the framework with an understanding of the timeline and phases through which the diffusion of innovation and change occurs (Rogers, 2003). Also vital to beginning the development or re-developing assessment processes is an understanding of likely sources of objections and ways to resolve those objections (see Hutchings, 2010, above), how to ensure momentum to achieve successful implementation, and how to sustain assessment processes.
- *Involve relevant stakeholders in a needs assessment phase*
  - *Create mechanisms for faculty dialogue and input about assessment.* Develop and utilize internal social media sites to develop dialogue, especially with part-time faculty. Town halls, periodic online forums, faculty focus groups, and brown-bag lunches on assessment are some other ideas. Engage faculty formal and informal leaders in dialogue.
  - *Involve the students.* Bringing student government organizations into the planning phase will help with acceptance and active involvement in assessment. Structured peer review and co-development of assessment rubrics and instruments with students are also successful strategies (Palomba and Banta, 1999).
  - *Involve and seek input from other stakeholders as appropriate.* Besides faculty and students, advisory committees, external employers, members of the community and the board of trustees are all likely candidates for inclusion.
  - *Define needed goals for assessment.* What will the institution do with information derived through assessment? How will the institution define its own internal standards, and will those be fixed or flexible standards?
  - *Define user information needs.* Use information gathered through dialogues to define user needs. Validate information collected, user needs for information defined, and how assessment may be linked to those needs.
  - *Define suitable institutional vocabulary.* Defining a suitable institutional vocabulary for assessment that honors the institutional culture and for which faculty can take ownership.
- *Define needed elements of the assessment system*
  - *Engage faculty leadership* and modify extant organizational structures to provide room for assessment or create new structures: Work with the faculty governance structure to include the work of

assessment in planning committees, curriculum committees, assessment, planning, and institutional effectiveness committees.
- *At the department level*: Create student learning outcomes at individual, course, program levels; assessment rubrics; assessment annual plans; student learning outcomes-based program review templates.
- *Faculty governance*: Update the charter of the curriculum committee and the general education committee to include assessment of student learning outcomes; create an assessment/institutional effectiveness committee if none currently exists.
- *Leverage extant organizational structures*: Develop and modify extant processes to explicitly include assessment information. Assessment should be an input to strategic planning processes; annual budgeting processes; resource allocation for evidence-based improvements in student learning based on program review or annual assessment findings, and from the findings of general education assessment.
- *Create the virtual organization.* Assessment has workload implications, even though they are tremendously mitigated by the use of appropriate technology. Sustainability is critical. No assessment system will survive if there is not a feasible way to assimilate and analyze assessment data. Create the virtual and personnel structure to carry out the work, within programs, departments and colleges.
- *Bring the champions together.* Sustainability is facilitated by finding, bringing together and giving public recognition to the champions, early adopters, and pockets of success already operating in the institution. They provide exemplars and paradigm pioneers for others to follow.
- *Provide support and professional development.* Provide abundant professional development opportunities and as-needed consultation on institutional effectiveness and program assessment. Create a support system for faculty, chairs, staff, and unit heads for implementing assessment.
- *Develop a communication plan.* Create a multi-level, longitudinal communication plan—like a development campaign—and use it as a master document. Craft situationally-appropriate messages derived from that master document. Social media groups and techniques should be a mainstay of the communication plan.
- *Begin Implementation*
  - Create a timeline with development milestones: Create a roll-out time line with milestones for development of various elements.
  - Implement according to the plan. Anticipate and plan for roadblocks to avoid breakdowns in the process.
- *Create a feedback system.* How is assessment working? What are the roadblocks? Creating a flexible, responsive feedback system will enable the assessment and institutional effectiveness system itself to self-regulate and improve.
- *Ensure sustainability.* Over time, seek to develop the 'culture of evidence' as an integrated part of core institutional infrastructure and processes, including:

- departmental retreats
- annual planning, budgeting, and reporting
- strategic planning
- academic calendar
- periodic program reviews
- budgeting at the college/institutional level
- performance management
- socialization processes for new faculty
- ongoing professional education opportunities for faculty
- integrate with faculty reward structure and provide recognition for good practices

Examples of Developed Plans

In this final part of the chapter, we provide two examples: one of a departmental assessment plan, and one of a college-level plan for an art and design institution. (Other examples can be found in the Case Studies chapter towards the end of this book.) Numerous other assessment and institutional effectiveness plans may be linked to from the website *Internet Resources for Higher Education Outcomes Assessment*, at http://www2.acs.ncsu.edu/UPA/archives/assmt/resource.htm.

One of the deliverables of an assessment system should be a feasible assessment plan at the program/department level across all degree programs. The plans should enable faculty and other readers to answer questions such as: What did faculty intend to measure, and at what competency level? What assessment methods did faculty decide to use, or to develop, and why? Have faculty set appropriate achievement goals and did students meet them? An example of a well-articulated and inclusive assessment plan for Fine Art at the University of Florida, at http://assessment.aa.ufl.edu/Data/Sites/22/media/2012-13uaap/2012-13uaap-fine-arts/2012-13-fine-arts-art-bfa-aap.pdf , contains an appropriate and comprehensive list of elements, including:

- Program-level statement of purpose or mission statement
- Statement of intended student learning outcomes
- Curriculum maps, one for each of the eight specializations
- Multi-year assessment timeline and cycle
- Statements of assessment methods and processes used
- Table of assessment oversight provided by faculty
- Three-year comparison and linkage of student learning outcomes focused on content knowledge, critical thinking, and communication
- Departmental rubric for assessing student work, focusing on student learning outcomes of content knowledge, critical thinking, and communication

At the college or institutional level, articulating shared and widely-understood conceptual models of how assessment information feeds into and becomes part of ongoing planning, review, curricular adjustment, budgeting, and the resource allocation process will serve as a communication vehicle to internal and external audiences of just how assessment is integrated into the fabric of the school or college, at the degree level through the college level. An example below from Otis College of Art and Design (Ballard, 2013) provides an overview of how an annual assessment cycle, periodic program review process, and regional accreditation operate in a coordinated manner to ensure the effective use of assessment information to pursue programmatic improvement and better learning outcomes for students.

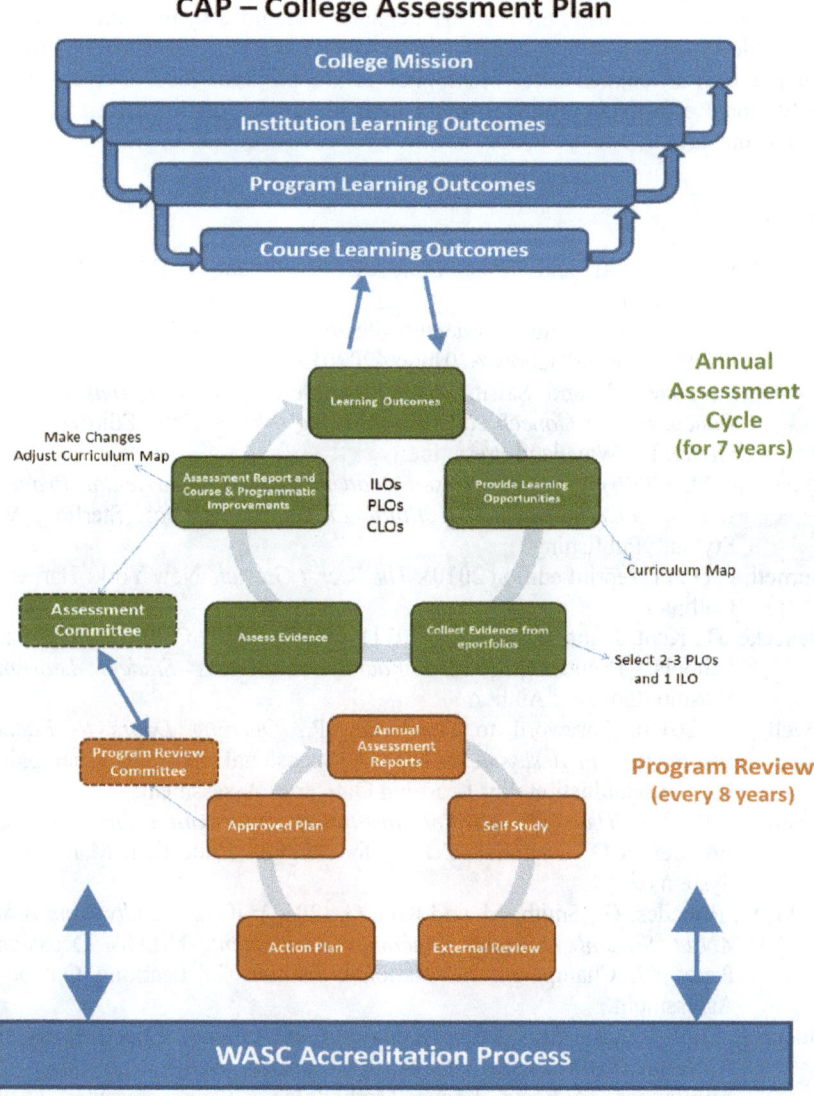

Figure 9.1: College assessment map.
Source: Ballard (2013).

Summary

Bringing together themes discussed in earlier chapters, this chapter has provided a roadmap and set of guidelines for the process of putting together an assessment system in the creative disciplines. Ways of systematically increasing faculty involvement in assessment were advanced. The organic and gradual development of a sustainable assessment program, from the individual student to the program, college, and institution level was detailed. The chapter included a discussion of change management, sources of resistance to beginning a program of assessment and other likely bumps in the road. The chapter concluded by providing direction in the development of a sustainable assessment program and characteristics of what a well-articulated assessment plan at the program level and a suitable institutional effectiveness model might look like in the context of creative and performing arts.

References

Ballard, D. (2013). Art and Design Colleges: Assessment on Their Own Terms. Retrieved from http://www.otis.edu/sites/default/files/Assessment%20on%20Their%20Own%20Terms%20rev%20June%202013.pdf.

Boone, E., Jones, J. and Safrit, R. (2002). *Developing Programs in Adult Education: A Conceptual Programming Model* (2nd Edition). Long Grove, IL: Waveland Press, Inc.

Bresciani, M. (2006). *Outcomes-Based Academic and Co-Curricular Program Review: A Compilation of Institutional Good Practices.* Sterling, VA: Stylus Publishing.

Burnett, F. (1911, reprint edition 2010). *The Secret Garden.* New York: Harper Collins.

Denecke, D., Kent, J. and Wiener, W. (2011), writing for the Council of Graduate Schools: *Preparing Future Faculty to Assess Student Learning.* Washington, DC: Author.

Ewell, P. (2010). Foreword to Hutchings, P., *Opening Doors to Faculty Involvement in Assessment.* NILOA Occasional Paper #4. Champaign, IL: National Institute for Learning Outcomes Assessment.

Ewell, P. (1984). *The self-regarding institution: information for excellence.* Boulder, CO: National Center for Higher Education Management Systems.

Gold, L., Rhoades, G., Smith, M. and Kuh, G. (2011). *What Faculty Unions Say About Student Learning Outcomes Assessment.* NILOA Occasional Paper #9. Champaign, IL: National Institute for Learning Outcomes Assessment.

Hoey, J. (1995). Assuring Faculty Input into Institutional Effectiveness and Assessment Processes at North Carolina State University: An Application of Focus Group Methodology. Paper presented at the Annual Forum of the Association for Institutional Research, Boston, MA.

Hoey, J. and Bosworth, S. (2009). Institutional Effectiveness: A New Back-to-

Basics Approach. Workshop presented at the 2009 meeting of the Southern Association of Colleges and Schools, Commission on Colleges.

Hutchings, P. (2010). *Opening Doors to Faculty Involvement in Assessment.* NILOA Occasional Paper #4. Champaign, IL: National Institute for Learning Outcomes Assessment.

Middaugh, M. (2009). *Planning and Assessment in Higher Education: Demonstrating Institutional Effectiveness.* Hoboken, NJ: John Wiley and Sons.

Palomba, C. and Banta, T. (1999). *Assessment Essentials: Planning, Implementing, and Improving Assessment in Higher Education.* Hoboken, NJ: John Wiley and Sons.

Rogers, E. (1995). *Diffusion of Innovations,* 4th Edition. New York: Free Press.

Suskie. L. (2009). *Assessing Student Learning: A Common Sense Guide*, 2nd Edition. Hoboken, NJ: John Wiley and Sons. Texas A&M International University, Office of Institutional Effectiveness and Planning (2010). Institutional Effectiveness Practitioner's Manual. Laredo, TX: Author. Retrieved from http://www.tamiu.edu/adminis/iep/documents/2010-TAMIU-IE- Practitioners-Manual.pdf.

Walvoord, B. (2010). *Assessment Clear and Simple: A Practical Guide for Institutions, Departments, and General Education*, 2nd Edition. Hoboken, NJ: John Wiley and Sons.

Chapter 10: Establishing a Value to Art and Assessment and then Explaining Them to Outsiders

The aim of education should be to teach us rather how to think, than what to think—rather to improve our minds, so as to enable us to think for ourselves, than to load the memory with the thoughts of other men.
— John Dewey

All of academia has entered a period of calls for more accountability. Despite billboard style advertisements from HSBC claiming, "Education is still the best investment," politicians and parents have been clamoring for colleges and universities to justify the cost of education; employers and accreditors have been demanding that colleges and universities state what a degree says students know and can do. "Demonstrating the value and relevance of these outcomes to an audience often inclined to view the academic and political realms as separate and distinct is one of our most daunting—and important—challenges" (Johnson & Gould, 2009, p. 34).

When one is trying to answer these accountability questions for an arts education, something that can seem by some people as being esoteric, challenges exist unlike in the fields of engineering and other sciences. How many times have students heard comments like "you're studying classical music performance, but what are you going to do when you graduate? I guess you could always teach," or "painting or acting is fine as a hobby, but how will you get a *real* job?" These comments often lead to well-meaning parents or other relatives (or even sometimes faculty when speaking with students who possess average talent) talking about transferable skills and how things learned during arts education (such as critical thinking and analysis) can be used in arts-related or even non-arts occupations.

But shouldn't faculty, staff, administration, and students in the arts be able to explain the value of arts to "outsiders?" Part of the assessment process in any discipline is putting the assessment results into a format that others—potential students, parents, politicians, and employers—can understand. In order to do that one needs to be able to explain what is assessed and why, to understand the difference between qualitative and quantitative findings, and to explain how this both summarizes current student learning and improves future students' education.

Assigning Value to Art

Lewis Hyde writes in his book *The Gift: Creativity and the Artist in the Modern World* (2009), "The art that matters to us ... is received by us as a gift is received. Even if we have paid a fee at the door of the museum or concert hall, when we are touched by a work of art something comes to us that has nothing to do with the price." And yet, artists, arts organizations, economists, educators, and even politicians have debated for eons the value of art—a single piece or production of art, the role of the arts in a society, and the worth of students studying art (both for the arts' and students' sakes and for its value to the rest of the students' educations). In his paper, "What values should count in the arts? The tension between economic effects and cultural value," economist Bruno S. Frey (2005) goes straight to the heart of the ongoing debate between economists and "arts people" (Frey's term). Frey reports that, "arts people focus more on the economic effects of the arts than economists do" and "arts economists concentrate more on the artistic aspects than arts people do" (p. 2).

Part of this could be because arts people are accustomed to having to justify their art or their artistic ideas to potential funders. Politicians and arts grants-makers might find Hyde's comment an inadequate justification for financial support, instead asking for economic and instrumental impacts, such as raised standardized test scores, revitalized communities, or fewer at-risk youth wandering the streets, and jobs created. Frey is quick to say that arts people take artistic value as a given; whereas, others may need to be persuaded of arts' benefits to society.

David Hume, in his essay "Of the Standard of Taste" (1706), attempts to explain the "nature of value judgments in the arts by means of an empirical, rather than a priori, relation" (Ward, 1998, p. 1). Hume's argument more than three hundred years ago states that a difference exists between sentiment and reason. Sentiment varies from person to person, but reason or "avowed principles of art" will be acknowledged by anyone educated or possessing "taste" (p. 4). T. S. Eliot, on the other hand, expresses that both understanding and sentiment are necessary to value art when he wrote, "It is certain that we do not fully enjoy a poem unless we understand it; and on the other hand, it is equally true that we do not fully understand a poem unless we enjoy it."

Is it true that sentiment and understanding the principles of art are necessary if one is assigning value to art? If one needs to possess both of these things, are they the only attributes necessary to "judge" art, and by extension, the value of arts education? Budd (1996) believes that the sentiment towards art must be felt as part of an intrinsic reward system for it to be adequately understood and valued. Additionally, Ward (1998) argues that discernment of design and psychological insight are required of an arts critic, or someone who is "in a position properly to exercise a delicacy of taste" (p. 2) before she or he can answer the crucial aesthetic question of "how imaginatively or creatively the artistic conventions are employed when the work is viewed as seeking to fulfill its purpose within its cultural milieu" (p. 5).

And this brings us to the one final consideration for assigning value to art: its role in the culture. Honig (2011) chronicles the changes in the value of arts when it went from a "gift-reward" to a commodity in the marketplace. Ivey (2011) purports that valuation in the arts is found in two extremes: the popular "art-as-a-commodity," and the precious "art-is-what-you-need-even-if-you-don't-want it."

Regardless what criteria one chooses to use to assign value to art and arts education, these criteria must be clearly spelled out in the assessment instruments, to those being assessed, and to those trying to understand the results of the assessment.

Assigning Value to the Assessment of Arts

In their 2009 paper "Measuring Intrinsic Value: How to Stop Worrying and Love Economics," Bakhshi, Freeman, and Hitchen write, "Stop insisting that intrinsic benefits cannot be measured, and start demanding that they should be...Cultural economics strengthens the case for the arts in ways that have not been taken seriously until now."

Hume (1706) almost made the case for assessment of the arts without calling it as such when he said that when we show a critic or a skeptic "an avowed principle of art" and then we illustrate this principle by examples that the person "must conclude upon the whole...every beauty and every blemish" (p. 4). It is the purview of those in arts education to ensure those outside the academy understand the purpose (value) of assessment, understand every blemish and every beauty in the education of arts students, and subscribe meaning to what the assessment data show.

The Alaska Department of Education succinctly sums the purpose of assessment: to improve learning. "It does this by:

- informing students, parents, and teachers of individual and group progress toward meeting the standards;
- demonstrating to students, parents, and the community the types of learning and levels of achievement sought;
- making possible comparisons involving student achievement across time, and when desired, among students, districts, or states;
- providing information to policy-makers at all levels to aid in decision-making" (p. 3).

In many ways this whole book has been devoted to explaining why arts assessment is important and how it can add value to the entire educational process.

Explaining Arts Assessment to Outsiders

Just as program notes explain the history and value of a piece of music to the audience and written explanation in the form of an artist's statement often accompanies art on display, providing written or digital explanation (text, graphs, charts, spreadsheets) of what is being assessed, how its value is established, its context, and the results of the assessment of creativity is imperative to any reader's or evaluator's understanding. In order to do these things the assessment methods themselves may need to be explained to the accreditors, granting organizations, or anyone else looking at the assessment results. After all, numbers in a vacuum are relatively meaningless when it comes to assessment, or as the authors of the Alaska Arts Framework warn: "Caution is needed in interpreting assessment results; assessment results are only approximations of the complete truth" (p. 4).

Farmer and Napieralski (1997) write, "Effective assessment must begin with real concerns of the stakeholders and result in useful information and recommendations related to the purpose of assessment." So the first thing outsiders need to understand is what was the purpose or goal of the assessment. Assessment can serve many different purposes. Continuous assessment takes place during the course of many visual and performing arts activities and gives the professor information on the student's level of involvement, on his/her stage and rate of development, and on immediate learning needs. As this book states in the Technical Foundations chapter, assessment can be objective or standardized, external, direct, indirect, or passive (or any combination thereof) and any of these methods could have similar or different goals. Assessment can also be formative or summative, and these types of assessments usually have very distinct goals. Formative assessments are designed "to contribute to student learning through the provision of information about performance" (Yorke, 2003). Formative assessment is useful for capturing and recording continuous progress and development (Brown, 1999). Formative types of assessment also help faculty to plan the next step in the student's learning and may suggest modifications to aspects of the arts curriculum—and these modifications may be different from term to term, based on the composition and skillset of the students in the course. Summative assessment, in contrast, concludes and encapsulates students' work or the assessment may pay attention to convergent thought (Johnson & Gould, 2009).

In addition to understanding the goal of the assessment activity, outsiders need to understand and acknowledge that arts assessment has a qualitative nature that evaluation in other disciplines may not possess. "One rigorous methodology common to the arts and humanities is qualitative field research, the aim of which is to validate findings through a range of interpretive strategies, no one of which is entirely sufficient in isolation" (Johnson & Gould, 2009, p. 34). Or Campbell & Scott-Kassner (2006) put this idea another way when they write, "Assessments do not necessarily involve quantification of data, and they provide an alternative to the somewhat narrow approach offered by traditional tests in order to report student achievement."

The next thing that must be understood by those outside the academy is how the assessment activities were conducted and by whom. "Assessments are not limited to teacher-based feedback; peer assessments and self-assessments are practical and effective alternatives that allow other sources to provide feedback on student progress. Therefore, assessing student progress using multiple measures of achievement provides educators with more flexible and sophisticated tools than do factual tests" (Johnson & Gould, 2009, p. 35). Arts assessment may not be a single assessment on one particular artifact. As an example, in the 3-D Design portfolio:

> Students are required to submit a specified series of images of their 3-D artworks and their artworks are evaluated independently according to their quality (demonstration of form, technique, and content), breadth (demonstration of visual principles and material techniques), and concentration (demonstration of depth of investigation and process of discovery). Using a well-delineated scoring rubric for each of these three areas, from three to seven artist-educators evaluate the submitted images of the artwork. The portfolios that are submitted are standardized in that specific instructions are provided to students that specify what type of artwork is appropriate and the students are provided with detailed scoring rubrics that delineate what is expected for each of the dimensions being assessed. (Lane, 2010, p. 6).

Assessment in arts disciplines is frequently and effectively conducted by experts or masters in the fields or by peers, as illustrated in Eisner's connoisseurship model (1976) discussed earlier in this book. This is another thing that sets assessments in arts disciplines apart from many academic areas of study.

Another thing that sets arts assessment apart from other fields, and which may not be readily apparent to those not in an arts discipline is that arts assessment tends to be ongoing. "Assessment in the visual arts takes place as the child engages in the creative process of making art, when a piece of art work is completed and while making a personal response to art works. This approach to assessment enables the teacher to ensure that the whole spectrum of visual arts education is reflected in the child's learning and in his/her teaching" (Government of Ireland, 1999). Arts education provides a multitude of assessment points that cover a whole host of assessment objectives.

Once the goals and methods of the assessment are understood, one must explain the results. Results can be anything from the evaluation of student work or portfolios to licensure exam pass rates (such as those for Interior Design and Architecture or teacher credentialing programs). For example, in a successful juried musical performance, an effective response in the audience can be assessed in addition to psychomotor skills and a cognitive understanding of the music that combine to form a moving or convincing performance, or what Seels and Glasgow (1990) refer to as an internalized affect for the idea or an emotional commitment to the work.

The University of Massachusetts Amherst, in its handbook *Course-Based Review and Assessment: methods for understanding student learning*, recommends in Chapter 6: Interpreting and Using the Results of Classroom Assessment that reports to outsiders should cover five main components of assessment:

1. the goals and objectives you established for your course
2. the assessment methods you chose or designed
3. what you found out about student learning in your classroom
4. how these findings are being used for improvement
5. action to take (p. 46)

The handbook authors recommend using an assessment matrix like this one, adapted from Palomba & Banta (1999):

Table 10.1: Sample assessment matrix.

Goals/Objectives	Method	Results	Interpretation	Action to Take

Source: Adapted from Palomba & Banta (1999).

Other formats for explaining assessment results to outsiders include the methods created by Harvard Graduate School of Education's Project Zero, where faculty and students, employed the Studio Thinking Framework to develop e-portfolios as part of the Online Arts Assessment Project. (One example created by a K-12 teacher in Alameda, California, can be viewed at www.ccsesaarts.org/content/TeacherPages/johnson/assessment.html). The Stanford Center for Assessment, Learning, and Equity (SCALE), in its *Visual Arts Assessment Handbook*, also provides clear instruction (geared more towards primary and secondary schools but easily adapted to higher education) on pages 38 through 40 of their booklet, found at http://www.molloy.edu/Documents/Education%20Division/edTPA_VSA_Handbook.pdf . These instructions advise the inclusion of information about the unique composition of your student body or the characteristics of the setting of the assessments, any special equipment used during the assessments, and commentary on any artifacts you are attaching as samples of student work. Just be sure if you are including actual student work that you have release forms from the students and any fellow faculty members (whether you use their names or not), as mentioned under the Protection of Human Subjects part of the Technical Foundations chapter.

Other, more holistic assessment reports can be found on Portland State University's website at http://www.pdx.edu/unst/university-studies-assessment-reports. Seven pages of Senior Capstone Assessment report is displayed on the website. This assessment includes both quantitative and qualitative assessment measures and serves as a fine example of how one institution tells part of its story to constituents, and it answers the question of what its students know and can do. Included in this document is the final piece of information you want outsiders to understand: how your institution, program, and/or course is using the assessment results to create improvements to student learning and the student experience.

Summary

The value of art has been debated for centuries. David Hume (1706), Malcolm Budd (1996), and Andrew Ward (1998) have presented various standards and arguments for how to set a value to art based on sentiment, discernment of design, an intrinsic reward system, the inventiveness and/or imaginativeness of the employment of artistic conventions, and the work fulfilling its purpose in the cultural milieu. Assessment of arts education is the most effective way to explain the value of such education to accreditors, grant-making organizations, parents, politicians, media, and others on the periphery of academic circles.

But in order for these "outsiders" to understand assessment they must first understand how arts assessment differs from assessment in other disciplines, grasp the goals of assessment, what is being assessed and by whom, the methods used to assess, what the results are, most importantly what the results mean, and how those results will be used to enhance current and future student learning.

References

Alaska Department of Education & Early Development Arts Framework, Chapter 5: Assessment. (2013) Retrieved from http://www.educ.state.ak.us/tls/frameworks/arts/6assess1.htm

Bakhshi, H., Freeman, A., Hitchen, G. (2009). Measuring intrinsic value: how to stop worrying and love economics. MPRA Paper No. 14902. Retrieved from http://mpra.ub.uni-muenchen.de/14902/1/MPRA_paper_14902.pdf

Brown, S. Institutional strategies for assessment. In: Brown S. & Glasner A. eds. *Assessment matters in higher education: choosing and using diverse approaches*. Philadelphia: Society for Research into High Education and Open University Press: 1999. Ch. 1.

Budd, M. (1996). *Values in Art*. London, UK: Penguin Books.

Campbell P.S., Scott-Kassner C. (2006) *Music in childhood, third edition*. Belmont, CA: Thompson-Schrimer.

Eisner, E. (1976). Educational Connoisseurship and Criticism: Their Form and Functions in Educational Evaluation. *Journal of Aesthetic Evaluation*, 10 (3-4): 135-150.

Farmer, D. W., Napieralski, E. A. (1997). Assessing learning in programs. In Handbook of the undergraduate curriculum, J. G. Gaff & J. L. Ratcliff (Eds.). San Francisco: Jossey Bass, pp. 591-607.

Frey. B. S. (2005). What values should count in the arts? The tension between economic effects and cultural value. Center for Research in Economics, Management, and the Arts (CREMA). Working Paper 2005-24. Retrieved from http://www.crema-research.ch/papers/2005-24.pdf.

Government of Ireland. *Visual Arts Education Curriculum*. (1999). Retrieved from http://www.curriculumonline.ie/en/Primary_School_Curriculum/Arts_Education/Visual_Arts/Visual_Arts_Curriculum.pdf

Honig, E. (2011). Honor, art, and excellence in early modern europe." *Beyond Price: Value in Culture, Economics, and the Arts*. Cambridge, U.K.: Cambridge University Press.

Hume, D. (1706). Of the standard of taste. *English Essays: Sidney to Macaulay*. Vol. XXVII. The Harvard Classics. New York: P.F. Collier & Son, 1909–14; Bartleby.com, 2001. Retrieved from www.bartleby.com/27/.

Hutter, M., Throsby, D. ed. (2007) *Beyond Price: Value in Culture, Economics, and the Arts*. Cambridge, U.K.: Cambridge University Press.

Hyde, L. (2009). *The Gift: Creativity and the Artist in the Modern World*. New York: NY: Vintage.

Ivey. B. (2011). Going to extremes: commercial and nonprofit valuation in the U.S. arts system. *Beyond Price: Value in Culture, Economics, and the Arts.* Cambridge, U.K.: Cambridge University Press.

Johnson R., Gould. C. (Spring 2009). Special challenges of assessing undergraduate research in the arts and humanities. *CUR Quarterly,* 29 (3), 33-38.

Lane, S. (2010). Performance assessment: The state of the art. (SCOPE Student Performance Assessment Series). Stanford, CA: Stanford University, Stanford Center for Opportunity Policy in Education.

Palomba, C. A., & Banta, T. W. (1999). *Assessment essentials.* San Francisco: Jossey-Bass

Seels, B. Glasgow, Z. (1990) *Exercises in Instructional Design.* Columbus: OH: Merrill Publishing Company.

Visual Arts Assessment Handbook. (2012). Stanford Center for Assessment, Learning and Equity (SCALE). Retrieved from http://www.molloy.edu/Documents/Education%20Division/edTPA_VS A_Handbook.pdf.

Ward, A. (1998). Putting value into art. *Π A I Δ E I A: Aesthetics and Philosophy of the Arts.* Retrieved from http://www.bu.edu/wcp/Papers/Aest/AestWard.htm.

Yorke, M. Formative assessment in higher education: Moves towards theory and the enhancement of pedagogic practice. *Higher Education.* 2003:45(4), 477-501.

Chapter 11: Case Studies

University of Nevada Las Vegas
Louis Kavouras, Chair, UNLV Department of Dance
College of Fine Arts
Department of Dance

Over the past ten years, the University of Nevada Las Vegas has been engaged in an active assessment process that has led to the implementation of more assessment practices and departmental dialogue. The university goal is the ongoing assessment of student learning.

In departmental discussions, the Department of Dance at UNLV decided that we should embrace assessment and find ways to make the process vital, useful, and robust. During these discussions, dance faculty realized several things--we found that we were assessing dance majors all the time: in Studio classes and rehearsals, in dance technique placement auditions, in scholarship auditions, in dance jury examinations, in choreographic showings and critiques, in auditions for concerts, and in portfolio and resume reviews. Some faculty jokingly stated that, "if it moved in the department, we assessed it."

The challenge with all of this performance assessment was how to capture the assessment information from each of these auditions, movement exams, and performances, and how to create a central place where faculty could access this information and use it.

In the Department of Dance, the dance jury examination is one of the chief assessment mechanisms. During this end of semester exam each dance major performs a ballet, modern, and jazz dance movement combination for the dance technique faculty. The exam is designed to allow technique faculty the opportunity to see students perform in the three departmental dance techniques. Faculty score each jury exam with a rubric of 1-5 (1- Unsatisfactory, 2- Needs Improvement, 3- Satisfactory, 4- Above Average, 5- Outstanding) in two areas, technique and performance. The exam also allows for written comments. Therefore each student would leave a jury exam with the following: six judges' scores in Ballet Technique, Ballet Performance, Modern Dance Technique, Modern Dance Performance, Jazz Dance Technique and Jazz Dance Performance. (Total of 36 scores plus comments)

CASE STUDIES

The exam presented a large data problem. Each of the department's 100 dance majors would enter the room holding six sheets of paper, which she or he would distribute to each faculty judge. Each judge would then watch the student perform and then write a score (1-5) on the paper. After the exam a six hundred page pile of these papers were then given to the department assessment coordinator whose task was to compile data and give an average in the six areas. Because of the magnitude of this job, even with a database, often the compilation of scores could not be achieved until well into the next semester. The data therefore was available for assessment report purposes, but was not immediately available for the student and for the teachers.

The idea for a solution was to digitize the entire process and remove the paper element. The goal was to develop a database system that allowed the department to schedule a jury exam. Faculty judges could then log onto this system, look up a student, and record the jury exam scores and comments. These would then immediately come together into a student average as well as a department mean. In theory this seemed like a simple and solvable process.

To solve the problem the department decided to use Filemaker Pro 12 software to create the database. This immediately led to the next dilemma; Filemaker Pro like many other database software solutions does not allow more than one user on any single record adapting that record at any given time. Six faculty judges could not enter data on the record of the student who was performing the jury. To solve this the department decided to employ a different strategy. Rather than one record, what if each judge was able to create his or her own record for the six scores. If the jury exam had a unique number then all six judges' scores could be brought together by the database onto an overall jury exam record for that unique number.

Here is a screen shot of this part of the database. The black lines show how the information is able to flow from the judges' database to the centralized jury exam database.

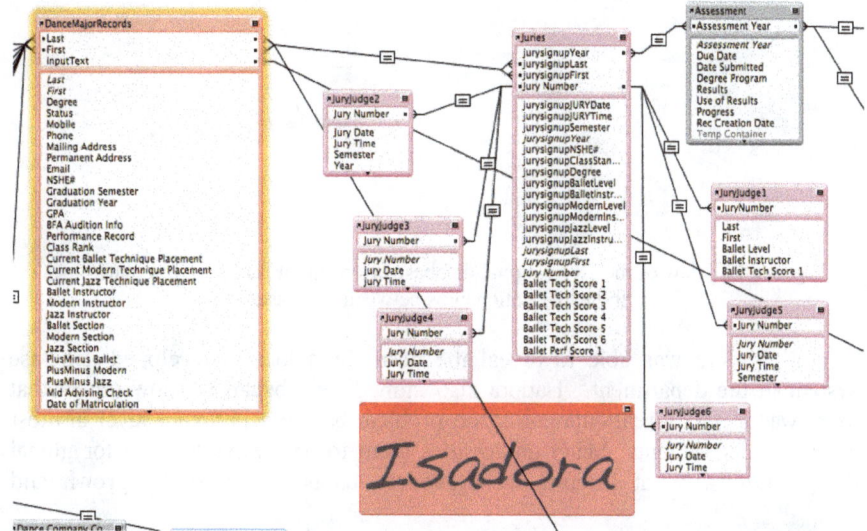

Figure 11.1 Assessment databases: six judge databases report data to a centralized juries database. This data is then able to be sent to the main dance major records database.

From the centralized jury exam database, information is then able to flow to a student record database. This allows for all the dance majors' jury exams to come together for viewing in one central place.

Once the department was able to make this database work, the jury exam problem was completely solved. It also illuminated the fact that many other assessments in the department could be captured with a much larger relational database system. As the database grew we realized that it needed a name. The department chose the name Isadora. Isadora Duncan was a turn of the century artist and dancer. She was interested in a freedom of expression and in a new kind of movement flow. Isadora seemed the perfect name and metaphor, because if this database worked well, it would allow for a new flow and expression of information in the department.

Some of the challenges for this kind of system early on were in building and designing it. After the system was built there was a need to obtain faculty buy-in to use it. Overall though, these hurdles seemed insignificant. Once individuals saw how well data was being collected and how available the data was once it was collected, all were sold on the need to use Isadora in the department. The department also bought all faculty new iPads, which allowed them to easily log into Isadora and collect and use the data she contained. The fact that faculty got iPads to use for classes, research, and choreographic work was incentive to use the new system.

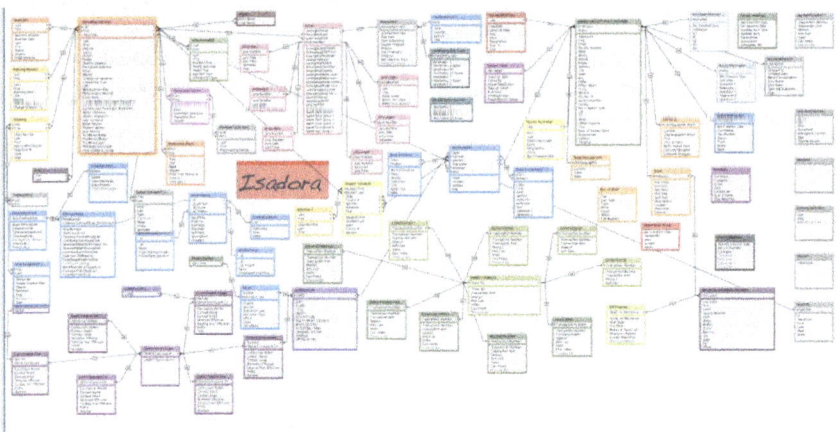

Figure 11.2 View of the 78 relational databases working in Isadora. Thin black lines indicate relationships between databases.

Overall Isadora was able to reveal the need for a locally-developed database system in the department. Isadora also immediately began to show others that there was in fact a real data collection problem on the department level in most academic departments. Many universities seem to be always looking for global data solutions. What Isadora has proved to us is that a locally grown and developed system is far more tailor-made and useful for the department. It is more customizable and can specifically address the needs of the department.

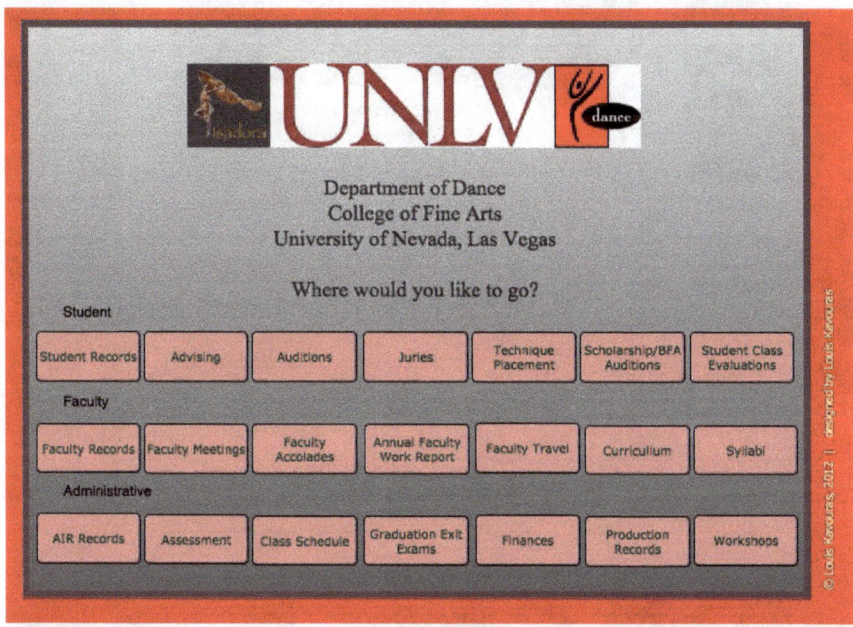

Figure 11.3: Opening screen of Isadora with buttons to take the user to the various subject areas.

As Isadora grew, she also was able to do more and more in the department. Faculty found they could e-mail all or specific populations of majors from within the database system, better than any other system currently available. In the design of Isadora, buttons were created on screen to automate and perform many tasks that faculty needed. Assessment of students was also enhanced due to the fact that faculty could now easily access and compare information that was previously less know and accessible. Faculty could see how well a student was being cast following auditions, what scholarships were being obtained over time, what classes were needed to graduate, and how well the student was progressing towards graduation. Additionally, when faculty advised a student, advising notes could be left in the student's record. All faculty members could then clearly see how their colleagues were advising majors and what was being advised. Suddenly there was a level of transparency that allowed all faculty to be aware of each other's interaction with majors. This has led to stronger levels of retention, progression and completion of majors in the program.

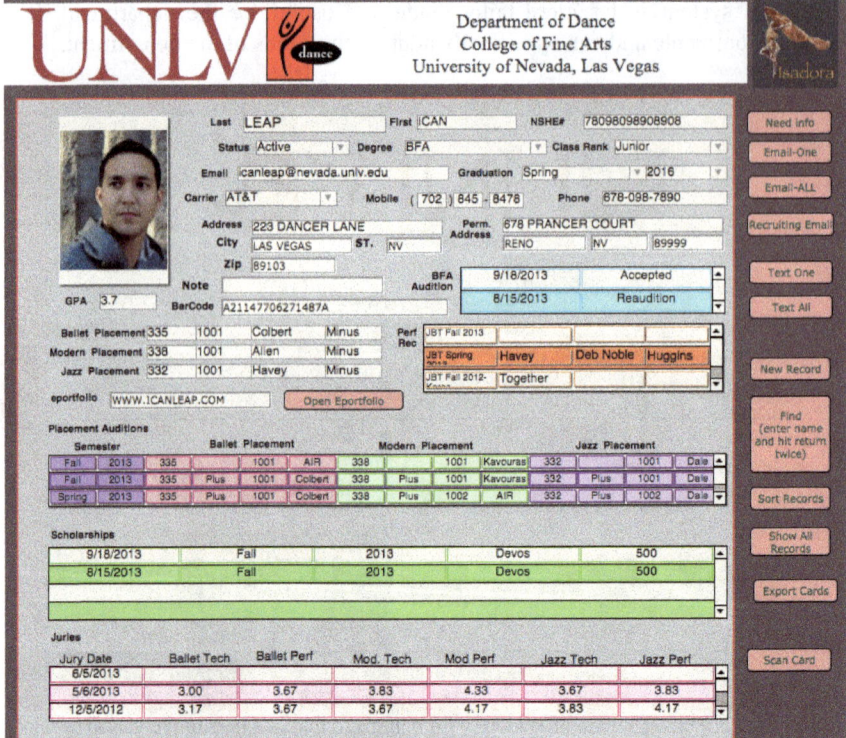

Figure 11.4 Screenshot from the dance majors database. Information from auditions and juries falls into the scrollable portals. The column on the right contains buttons that automate specific tasks the user might want to accomplish.

Beyond student data, Isadora is also able to capture information for faculty needs and concerns. Isadora began collecting data on faculty and was also able to manage the financial accounts and bookkeeping in the department, as well as fill out many forms. This proved that a centralized data system in the department went far beyond formative assessment; with time more and more of the departmental day-to-day operations were being accomplished and enhanced by Isadora.

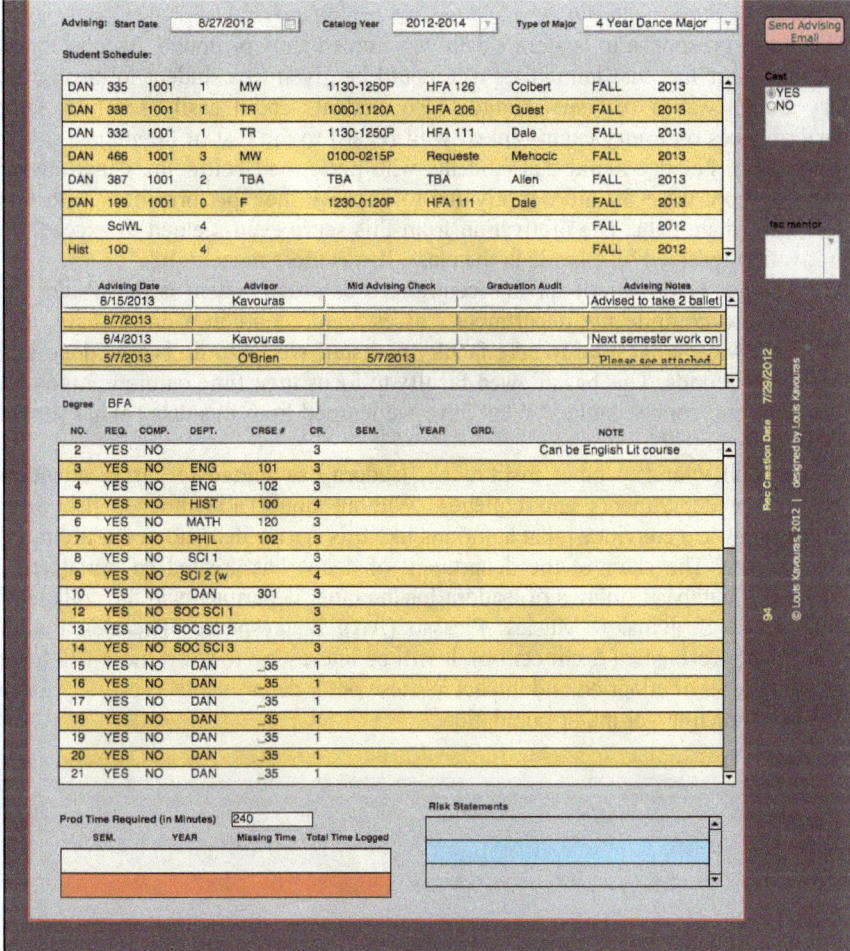

Figure 11.5 Student record showing advising information related to a students record, including, student schedule, advising meetings, and courses the student needs to graduate.

Figure 11.6 Jury exam data. Each column shows a judges technique and performance scores, followed by the students average score. The final column is the average score for all students who took the jury. On the bottom of the results is the students next semester technique placement.

The student response to Isadora's data was immediately profound. Faculty found that the sheer fact that immediate data could be given to a student following the jury exams was a real see-change. Also students could easily see how their performances on a jury exam ranked with regard to the rest of the majors in the department. Faculty found that students who performed below the departmental average score were far more motivated to improve their performances with this new immediate data. The motivation from this score even seemed to exceed the motivation received by a grade in the class. It was more meaningful.

Another great benefit for this centralized database system is that Isadora is now able to compile the department's assessment report in a quick, easy, and effortless way. What used to take faculty and staff weeks to do is now done in a matter of seconds. This has allowed faculty to focus their time on more important questions and concerns like, "What have we learned from this data? What should we do differently?"

At UNLV and at other institutions, Isadora has started to garner attention from other departments and colleges. Without doubt all who see her work immediately are convinced that solutions like this are needed and necessary in all departments. The chair of the department of dance has created an initiative to create five database siblings of Isadora for the other departments in the college of Fine Arts: Stravinsky (Music), Picasso (Art), Shakespeare (Theatre), Fellini (Film), and Corbusier (Architecture). It will be interesting to see if these will have the same level of adoption and impact in these other departments, especially those that have much larger major populations.

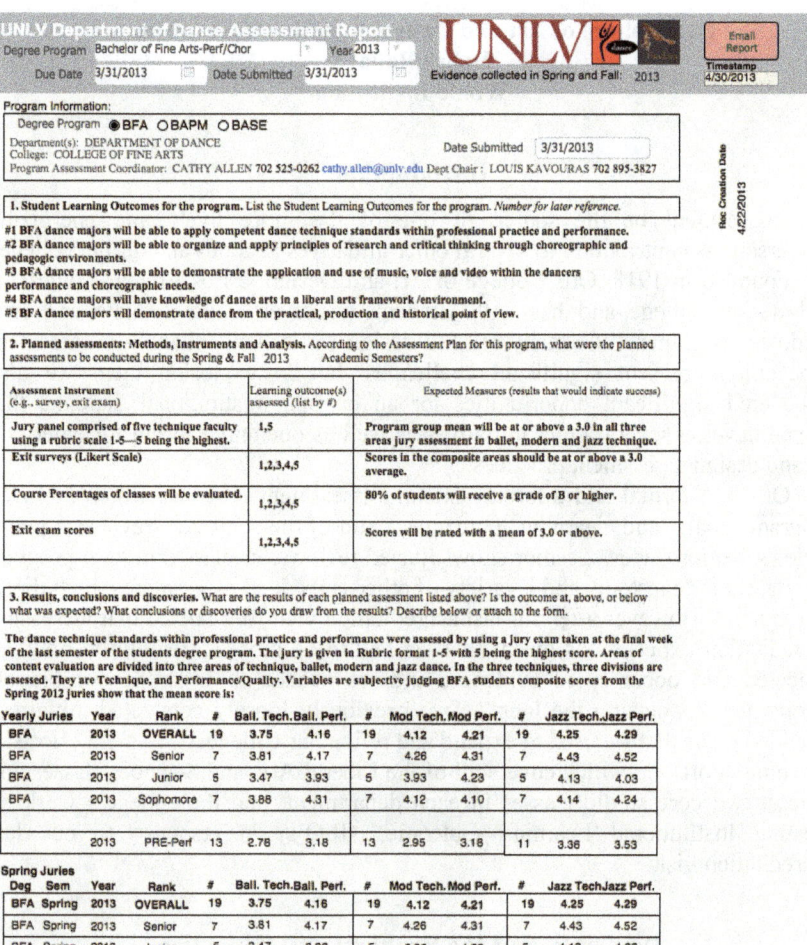

Figure 11.7 Screen shot from first page of Assessment report. Scores are tallied automatically.

Otis College of Art and Design Assessment Case Study,
Debra Ballard
Whole Institution

Introduction

Can assessment be the source of one of the more lively and energizing conversations contributing to several other initiatives at an art and design college?

Founded in 1918, Otis College of Art and Design is Los Angeles' oldest art and design college and has 1100 students in seven undergraduate and four graduate programs. Like many art and design institutions, changing assessment expectations present significant challenges, but in exploring them we also discovered significant opportunities for an ongoing institutional dialogue that helped develop several other initiatives as well as opening a forum for emerging art and design assessment practices.

Otis had formal and informal existing assessment practices which included program goals and learning outcomes, end-of-the-semester reviews, junior reviews, senior reviews, senior shows, juried reviews, in-class critiques, program review, senior capstone, and a variety of other embedded assessments, both direct and indirect. However after our last accreditation visit we realized that increasing accreditation expectations meant that we had to be more systematic in how we collected and documented evidence, and we needed to work on our biggest inconsistency, "closing the loop." Two previously loosely connected initiatives provided paths that we used to expand and refine our college assessment efforts: a Learning ePortfolio which covers all of the Liberal Arts and Sciences classes and at least two core studio classes in each department, and the college's work on creating Institutional Learning Outcomes (ILO's) in response to our last accreditation visit.

Description of the Problem and Objective

Our assessment challenges are similar to art and design programs. "There are specific disciplines, especially in the arts, in which developing outcomes appears to be at odds with the philosophy of the discipline" (Driscoll and Wood, p. 9). Can a medium sized, enrollment-driven nonprofit art and design institution create a meaningful and sustainable assessment infrastructure that is embedded in its daily activities that helps improve teaching and learning and addresses increasing accreditation expectations?

After our last successful accreditation visit, changes in the provost's office left our assessment effort unshepherded while our accreditor was redesigning the whole process. Initially somewhat reluctant, with our provost's gentle prodding I decided to attend the WASC Assessment Leadership Academy, a nine-month program that develops assessment leaders, which turned out to be a crucial part of working with the new provost to create and implement a college-wide assessment plan. A motivating apprehension was that failure to be proactive in this area could lead to externally imposed assessment methods like standardized testing. My project was to research and propose a college assessment plan and then work through the Assessment Committee to refine and implement it.

Challenges to Solving the Problem and Reaching the Objective

One major challenge to assessment at an art and design college is faculty concerns that accreditation assessment will compromise the innovative and creative outcomes essential to an art and design institution. The next considerable challenge is whether creativity can be broadly defined and then assessed across the disciplines. "Investigation showed widespread disagreement among the various design and creative arts disciplines (within the University and beyond) on what constitutes creativity and what constitutes creative ability; whether creative ability could or should be reduced to quantifiable parameters for assessment" (Cowdry and Williams, p. 1). We also had to define and assess our newly adopted Institutional Learning Outcomes. Otis has a large part-time faculty and a comparatively small academic administration so these strategic questions are always framed against the precious element of time and balance with many, many other demands. We wanted to be mindful as to how we could create a dynamic assessment structure that could flexibly address the needs of an art and design education that accommodates the inherent tension between what we do in constantly reformulating outcomes and boundaries and the more structured and sometimes static demands of accreditation.

Strategies, Creative Ways of Solving, and Reaching the Objective

Rather than reinventing the wheel or adding activities, expanding on existing practices and initiatives was critical to addressing the challenges in an embedded and sustainable way. Serendipitously we had also begun a Student Success effort that included credit and course reduction, which called for careful consideration of learning outcomes and a culture shift in how we looked at student success across the college. As part of this effort Academic Affairs was merged with Student Affairs, Registration, Financial Aid, and Admissions and the assessment effort became interwoven throughout the college to include those groups as well as several other academic support units through workshops and presentations. Our existing learning e-portfolio initiative had a reflective component and an unused assessment module, and assessment of our newly formed ILO's (creativity, skill and technique, collaboration, visual literacy, and social responsibility along with the new WASC Core Competencies of written and oral communication, critical thinking, information literacy, and quantitative reasoning) required that we look at how we define and assess these elements. We have been using the AAC&U's VALUE rubrics as a starting point as we define outcome levels within the institution. We found that having one department pilot initiatives and then using those efforts as models to scale was an efficient approach. Shifting attitudes from a culture of external compliance of assessment (though this never fully recedes attesting to external increasing expectations of accountability and transparency) to a path of achieving student success and improving teaching and learning was essential. Faculty attitudes toward accreditation and assessment range from hostile to inspired, but faculty are always interested in improving student learning.

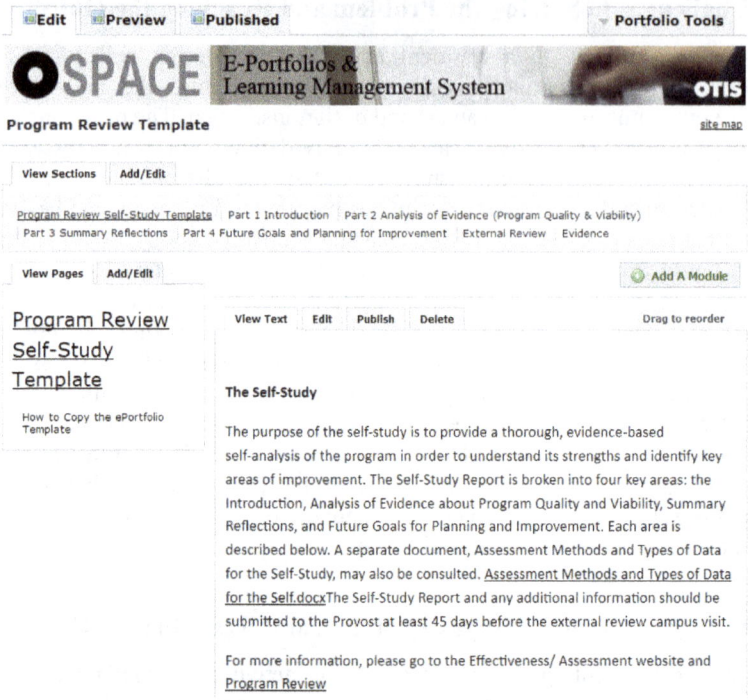

We closed the loop through the College Assessment Plan and the newly reconstituted Assessment Committee who review the results of the programs' annual assessment of 2-3 Program Learning Outcomes/Institutional Learning Outcomes and Program Reviews. For reporting ease and consistency, we created templates for the programs to use and an e-portfolio template for revised Program Review. The creation of a website that serves as a resource for faculty and administrators provided the necessary point of convergence to support assessment. It put all the information in one organized place. The call for transparency through a curriculum map became a vehicle for the part-time faculty because they could more easily see where their classes fit in our programs. Having one assessment leadership champion embedded in an administrative position (department chair) turned out to be advantageous in expediting the effort. The Assessment Leadership Academy proved key to addressing the challenge of time for creating the plan. Not only did it turn out to be an outstanding experience in both its content and meeting many delightful colleagues committed to addressing similar challenges, it provided that shelter from the "tyranny of time" and everyday demands to thoroughly research what worked best for our institutional needs.

Lessons Learned, Changes Made, and Accomplishments

Undertaking a college-wide assessment plan can at first seem overwhelming, but finding a group who are open to looking at teaching and learning, starting small and momentarily forgetting accreditation, and focusing on assessment as something we always do to improve student learning makes it so much more manageable and meaningful. We learned that when we see assessment as a collective conversation supporting student success and learning across departments as well as studio and liberal studies, faculty and administrators are much more willing to participate and have valuable contributions. Part of that process was developing a shared language to discuss assessment and our learning outcomes. We also learned that the whole enterprise framed an ongoing conversation as we moved into significant curricular reform. It became a venue to discuss our recently adopted Institutional Learning Outcomes, the possibilities for interdisciplinary and curricular/co-curricular cross-overs, credit reform and reduction, and seeing more possibilities for integrating theory and practice. In surveying where our ILO's existed in our programs, we got a better sense of many of the points of convergence that already exist within the college. We are now reviewing the literature in art and design assessment to see if we can improve upon our art and design practices with an expanded assessment model that balances quantitative and qualitative assessment as well as process and product.

By refining and coordinating our existing assessment practices already embedded in our ongoing review cycle, extending the existing eportfolio initiative, completing an institutional learning outcomes effort, and creating a curriculum map, our refined assessment plan addresses changing accreditation requirements, but more importantly, focuses on improving student learning and success. The reorganized Assessment Committee and revised Program Review process also serve as opportunities to engage faculty and chairs in discussions about curricular crossovers and emerging best practices in art and design assessment.

Conclusion

While we still have a range of attitudes toward assessment, we never anticipated that assessment could have been the start of stimulating, occasionally contentious, and always productive dialogue. The effort started conversations that have helped us better understand the common points and divergences that exist in our programs.

Because art and design assessment is comparatively overlooked in the assessment literature, it presents a welcome opportunity for us to continue the conversation and extend it. Having already completed a review of the literature for the Assessment Leadership Academy, we are looking at how we can better articulate distinctive elements of art and design assessment. Our future efforts will try to improve on our current assessment through a revised art and design model, particularly in the areas of Schon's use of reflection, process, and product, problem-based learning, creative thinking, elements of hard skills, soft skills, content knowledge, and approaches to learning and doing which complement our ILO's. The demands for accountability and transparency are not going away and are likely to increase. However, rather than just another imposition, it is an opportunity to make time to meet with colleagues for an interdisciplinary dialogue learning more about we do and how we might do it better.

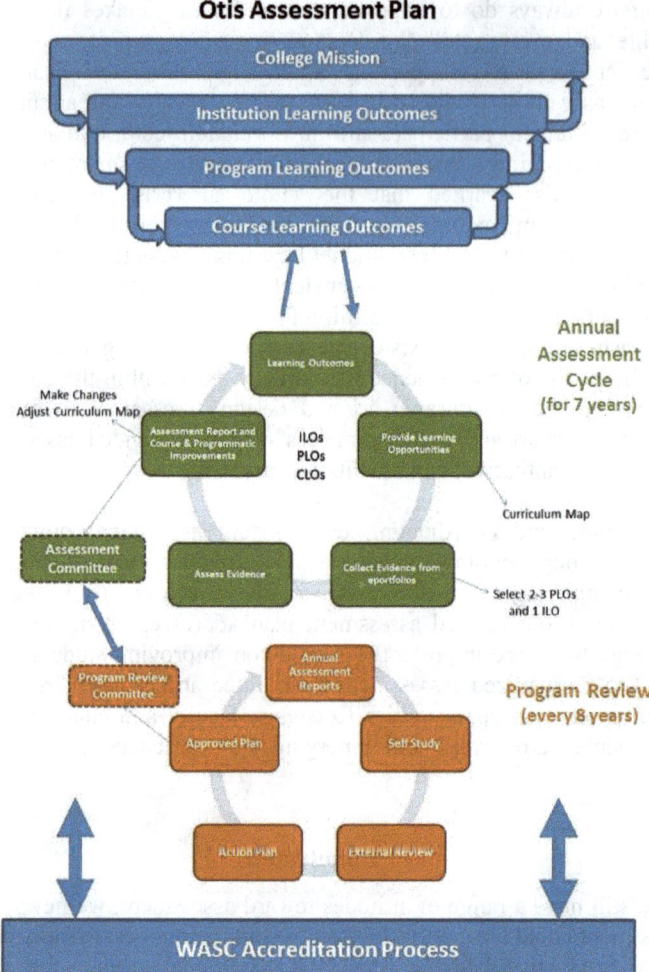

References

Cowdry, R. and Williams, R. (2007) "Assessing Creativity in the Creative Arts." Art, Design, and Communication in Higher Education 5.2: 97-117.

Driscoll, A.M., and Wood, S. (2007) Developing Outcomes-based Assessment for Learner-Centered Education. Virginia: Stylus Publishing,

Schon, D. A. (1983) Educating the Reflective Practitioner. USA: Basic Books.

Assessment, Curricular Reform, and Reassessment: University of Cincinnati Case Study
Alexander Christoforidis and Anton Harfmann
University of Cincinnati, School of Architecture and Interior Design (SAID)
Student evaluations by employers informing curricular adjustment over eight years

Introduction

The University of Cincinnati has used the cooperative education model for degrees leading to design and engineering professions for over 100 years. All of the academic programs involving design disciplines, including architecture, were founded with the cooperative education model. The cooperative education model requires alternating periods of academic work and paid professional work. During periods of professional work, students evaluate their own performance, and employers (supervisors) evaluate the work of the students they employ. The University of Cincinnati has developed its own web-based evaluation program, which allows for analysis or employer and student feedback.

Description of the Problem and Objective

Our particular study involved the analysis of architecture students' ability to understand design detailing for preparation of construction documentation. This is a skill that is fundamental to the execution of an architectural design. At the professional architectural firms that employed University of Cincinnati students, this type of work has been prepared in a digital format exclusively since 2002. Between the early 1980s and the early 2000s architectural firms were converting to a digital format, and by 2002 there were no firms who employed UC architecture co-op students and prepared construction documents by hand.

Between 2002 and 2005, an issue had been brought to the faculty's attention in the form of comments from both students and employers indicating that students' understanding of building construction fundamentals was lacking to some degree.

To quantify these assertions, questions were written for inclusion in the employer evaluation form that is sent to employers near the end of each student's cooperative education term in the format shown below:

Survey form of supplemental questions

Thinking about this student, please rate him/her on the following **building construction** performance skills.

The performance skills should be rated using the following scale.
5 = Excellent (the best or one of the best in this category)
4 = Good (above average but not excellent)
3 = Satisfactory (average when compared to others in this category)
2 = Poor (lacking in some important aspects or less than satisfactory)
1 = Unsatisfactory (lack of ability, failure to use it, or any other cause)
N/A = Not applicable or no opportunity to observe

Building Construction

Rating Scale

	5	4	3	2	1	N/A
a. Effectively uses digital technologies to represent building construction.	○	○	○	○	○	○
b. Understands the complexity of building construction.	○	○	○	○	○	○
c. Understands the complexity of detailing.	○	○	○	○	○	○
d. Understands how modeling and drawing translate into a structure.	○	○	○	○	○	○

[Courtesy, Division of Professional Practice and Experiential Learning, University of Cincinnati]

These questions continue to be used in our web-based assessment tool in this format through the end of 2013, and can be found at www.uc.edu/propractice/pal. Analysis of co-op employer evaluations was used to verify that this area of the curriculum did indeed warrant some type of intervention, and that adjustments made to two courses— "Construction methods and materials" and "digital skills"—would directly benefit the students in both academic and practice realms. The objective was to address pedagogical needs and employer concerns at the same time. Our cooperative education program works on the premise that higher student performance on the job leads to more learning opportunities.

Challenges to Solving the Problem and Reaching the Objective

Using employer feedback as a way of driving curricular adjustments was new to the academic faculty, and took some effort in convincing them that there was value in it. We made three points to the faculty: 1) The co-op program, and the evaluation system, put us in a unique position to collect and use employer input. 2) The vast majority of employers had also completed Professional Architectural degrees, so they had a good understanding of the academic requirements – in fact some were SAID alumni. 3) The faculty still own the curriculum. Therefore, if no reasonable conclusions could be drawn from employer input the faculty did not have to make adjustments. The challenge was to find a way to deliver the course material that would improve student performance on the job. Constructing the curriculum to satisfy both the points raised by the employers and the larger pedagogical goals of the curriculum was challenging. In the end, using co-op employer feedback to drive curriculum changes was accepted as worthy of consideration.

Strategies, Creative Ways of Solving, and Reaching the Objective

After deliberating possible curricular adjustments, SAID faculty decided on a strategy of combining the two courses (Construction methods and materials and the digital skills course) and sharing resources. This strategy allowed our students to use their newly acquired digital skills to draw construction details much in the same way they might be drawing construction details in a professional architectural firm. It gave purpose to the digital drawing exercises assigned to students, while allowing construction details to be composed with the precision that the digital format inherently offers. The syllabus and instruction schedule was rewritten for both courses. Once the adjustment was made, subsequent employer evaluations were re-assessed to see if there was a measureable difference in student performance. Since classes were split into two sections, one which worked as co-op students in the spring and one which worked as co-op students in the summer quarter, the classes were taught in the usual way in the Winter quarter of 2005 for "section I", but in the Spring quarter, the classes were combined for "section II".

2005	Group I	Group II
Effectively uses digital technologies to represent building construction	4.27	4.26
Understands the complexity of building construction	3.78	3.81
Understands the complexity of detailing	3.52	3.56
Understands how modeling and drawing translate into a structure	4.08	3.91

Table 2 – source: Leveraging Cooperative Education to Guide Curricular Innovation: The Development of a Corporate Feedback System for Continuous Improvement, 2008 Chapter 4, p.77. Center for Cooperative Education Research and Innovation, University of Cincinnati, Cincinnati, Ohio

Lessons Learned, Changes Made, and Accomplishments

The initial results did not show a significant change; however, more recently, the results were tracked for subsequent years, with sample sizes that were significantly higher than the initial study. We found that results continued to improve as the courses continued to be taught in the same combined manner. Of the four questions used, there was a marked (statistically significant) improvement in terms of effective use of digital technology, understanding the complexity of building construction and detailing (increases in the averages between 2005 and 2010 improved between .23 on question 1, .50 for question 2 and .60 on question 3). In terms of how modeling and drawing translate into a structure (the fourth question), there was a slight decline (.09). This is one of the most difficult aspects of professional architectural work to grasp. It is known among architects that it takes years to learn the relationship between detailed construction documents and the completed structure. For now, the issue raised by the fourth question will require further investigation. In general, however, the employer ratings improved until 2010 at which time they reached a peak, but changes in the profession prompted another curricular change:

	2006	2007	2008	2009	2010
Effectively uses digital technologies to represent building construction	4.37	4.37	4.44	4.49	4.50
Understands the complexity of building construction	4.10	4.16	4.26	4.25	4.28
Understands the complexity of detailing	3.91	3.92	4.01	4.06	4.12
Understands how modeling and drawing translate into a structure	3.86	3.88	3.98	3.99	3.99

By 2011, architectural firms had begun to adopt building information modeling (BIM) software. This software represented a significant shift in how buildings were being drawn. Instead of creating digital line drawings, designers could create three-dimensional digital models, which could carry a great deal of information about the buildings that were being designed through it. According to a study by the Greenberg Group published in the April 2010 issue of *Architect Magazine*, about 34% of architectural firms had been using BIM software, and that number was on the rise. In general, the architectural faculty looks ahead with the intention of preparing students to be advanced technologically as they enter the profession. In light of the shift to Building Information Modeling, therefore, the digital skills class made the change from using AutoCAD to the BIM software package, Autodesk Revit.

The table below compares the results of 2010 with the results from the subsequent three years when the digital skills portion of the class was taught using the BIM Modeling software, *Autodesk Revit*.

	2010	2011	2012	2013
Effectively uses digital technologies to represent building construction	4.50	4.37	4.44	4.49
Understands the complexity of building construction	4.28	4.16	4.26	4.25
Understands the complexity of detailing	4.12	3.92	4.01	4.06
Understands how modeling and drawing translate into a structure	3.99	3.88	3.98	3.99

Initially there was a slight decline (.12 to .20) between 2010 and 2011, and a reversal back up approaching the 2010 numbers by 2013. This is likely because in 2011, many firms still utilized AutoCAD heavily while UC students were no longer as well prepared in that paradigm when they arrived at their first co-op. As more firms started using the BIM software this changed, and is reflected in the employer evaluation results.

Conclusion and Summary

Based on the success of this effort it seems that asking employers for curricular advice can be very useful. There were difficulties convincing faculty to participate. The initial suspicion that faculty would be offended by any process that allowed employers to affect curriculum was confirmed. This hurdle was actually overcome while working on the project by temporarily suspending skepticism and allowing the work to progress. It soon became apparent that employers were much more interested in larger educational issues than making specific demands. In most cases, the employers themselves completed an architectural education before entering the profession, and they understood the pedagogical goals quite well. In addition, they had a much more direct benefit from students' critical understanding of construction methods and their translation to digital form.

It has been interesting to see the correlation between subsequent curricular adjustments, and the resulting evaluation scores. The data collected through a consistent evaluation tool allows for the study of cause and effect as it relates to curricular change. In this case, the following took place:

1. Questions were formulated and added to employer evaluations to study an issue raised by architectural employers and students.
2. Employer evaluation results were studied to confirm and quantify a suspected curricular weakness.
3. A curricular change was executed to address this weakness.
4. Evaluations were re-evaluated to study the effect of the curricular change, and the employer evaluation responses showed that the curricular change had a significant positive effect over the next four years.
5. A curricular adjustment was made in order to stay ahead of the technological curve. This was based not on employer evaluations, but on technological changes that were taking place throughout the architecture profession.
6. Evaluations showed a slight drop in employer response during the first year.
7. Continued study of employer evaluations showed a steady rise over the last two years.

The particular set of questions developed for this study can continue to be used to evaluate one aspect of the architectural curriculum, but what has become very clear during this study is the great potential for evaluating various aspects of curricula in cooperative education programs. The opportunity to collect and evaluate student performance in the controlled environment offered by a cooperative education program can be a very effective tool in the development of academic curricula.

University of the Pacific Conservatory of Music
Daniel Ebbers, Professor of Voice and Conservatory Faculty Director of Assessment
Assessment Planning for the Conservatory
(Professional school within the University of the Pacific)

Introduction

University of the Pacific is a comprehensive private California university consisting of a main campus in Stockton, the McGeorge School of Law in Sacramento, and the Dugoni School of Dentistry in San Francisco, California. There is a total enrollment of approximately 6,400 students enrolled across all three campuses. The Conservatory is one of seven schools and colleges located on the main campus in Stockton, and offers Bachelor of Music and Bachelor of Arts degrees in Music Composition, Music Education, Music History, Music Management, Music Therapy, Jazz Studies, and Performance degrees in orchestral strings, brass, woodwind, and percussion instruments, piano, and voice. There is also a Master of Music degree offered in Music Education and a Master of Arts degree in Music Therapy. The Conservatory enrolls approximately 230 undergraduate and 20 graduate students each year.

The Conservatory is one of the 16 charter members of the National Association of Schools of Music (NASM). The curricular standards and guidelines put forth by NASM have been used to establish and modify the Conservatory curriculum since 1924. These guidelines have been used to develop learning objectives and outcomes that are in line with contemporary standards for training performing musicians, educators, industry professionals, and therapists.

Description of the Problem and Objective

The Conservatory began the process of developing and implementing a system to assess learning in 2010. The University tasked each school and college to develop assessment activity and report about that activity and about its system and alignment with institutional learning objectives and the accreditation standards of the Western Association of Schools and Colleges (WASC) by the fall of 2013.

Challenges to Solving the Problem and Reaching the Objective

Among the challenges to this process are:

- A significant and complex debate among music schools about the value of learning assessment in music in higher education
- A fear that a culture of assessment really means a culture of standardization
- Resistance to codifying student learning; concern that codification is limiting and constraining
- Deep concern that assessment cannot fully explain what it is music faculty do and the true nature of their work

- In contexts where there are more than one evaluator, such as a juried examination, there are obstacles in establishing and agreeing upon common language for evaluation and assessment

Describing what it is we do is extremely difficult, both to ourselves and to the outside world. Fundamentally, what we do with music involves making choices utilizing the skills sets that are obtained throughout the students' matriculation. These many elements or parts can be summarily evaluated and aggregated, but when combined do not necessarily equal the whole part of what is to be our goal. Ultimately, we would like students to achieve specific levels of competency in all or many of these elements based on their major that will provide them with a framework to create something unique. Within this framework, musicians create music that is not standardized but in ways we hope differ from incarnations of the past. What can be measured are the elements that comprise the framework. We have been told by the assessment culture that we must have defined outcomes that can be measured, evaluated, and improved if possible. In the creation of music, however, the ultimate goal of the learning process is to create a different result that is determined by the students' intentions, not the intentions of the program, its instructors, or of the curriculum. In short, numerical analysis only tells a portion of what the school of music accomplishes and is limited in the scope of information it can provide to external evaluators.

In the jury format, there can be potential obstacles in the creation and composition of rubrics. Where there are multiple evaluators, coming up with an agreed upon document to measure students is often a difficult and complicated task. Many evaluators come from different backgrounds, and from varying pedagogical perspectives and networks of influence. As a result, the process of coming to a final decision involves compromise from one or more of the evaluators on both content and form. One can assume, however, that the very process of assessment will in time expose the various weaknesses and strengths of these rubrics and ideally, revisions would be an ongoing part of the process of curricular improvement.

Strategies, Creative Ways of Solving and Reaching the Objective

First, the most recently published set of NASM guidelines were used as the primary resource in the construction of learning outcomes for all majors as well as curricular elements common to all programs (this includes core musical study in ear training, music theory, music history, ensembles, and individual applied study). From these outcomes, curricular maps were developed indicating in which courses and experiences outcomes are introduced and developed.

Each program level supervisor, along with other faculty members from each program provided these maps in preparation for WASC affirmation of accreditation as well as for the Conservatory's re-accreditation with NASM in the spring of 2014, and in anticipation for their utilization in the ongoing assessment system. Further work has been done in several programs to create rubrics for jury examinations, requisite skill sets, course syllabi, and capstone events. This very clear line between the resource of NASM guidelines and the implementation of assessment creates a distinct advantage for the faculty member seeking to include assessment in the curriculum.

As the Faculty Director of Assessment in the Conservatory, the implementation strategy I utilized was to first examine my own program, (Voice), to determine the areas strengths and weaknesses. Subsequently I worked with the voice faculty to implement several new rubrics that will serve to bring our program in line with the practices in place across the University. Due in large part to the work of my colleague Dr. Lynelle Wiens, the voice program is one of most ideal programs to examine because of the many tools already in place. Most notably, the Voice Area Handbook, (written by and updated yearly by Dr. Wiens) is an excellent model of outlining student expectations. This publication is given to each student along with a cover letter that explains the entire curriculum, student expectations, rules, etiquette, and many other key pieces of information help to prepare the student for academic success. The thought behind starting with the Voice area was to work closely with a program that I myself know very well in order to provide a template from which other programs might draw to implement their own assessment model that specifically suits their program's needs. This does not imply, however, that other programs in the COM are necessarily behind or ahead of the assessment curve. In the Music Education and Music Therapy programs, for example, there is ongoing and historical evidence of rigorous assessment.

In order to understand the quality of assessment from each program I developed a rubric to evaluate current assessment practices.

Criterion	Initial (1)	Emerging (2)	Developing (3)	Highly Developed (4)
Program Intentions	Program intentions are problematic, incomplete, overly detailed, inappropriate, or disorganized.	Program intentions include reasonable outcomes but do not specify expectations as a whole. Relevant institution-wide learning outcomes and/or disciplinary standards may be ignored.	Program intentions are a well-organized set of reasonable outcomes that focus on the key knowledge, skills, and values students learn the program. It includes relevant institution-wide outcomes, such as critical thinking or communication. NASM standards have been considered.	Program intentions are reasonable, appropriate, and comprehensive. Faculty have agreed on explicit criteria for assessing students' level of master of each outcome and are in line with NASM standards

Assessable outcomes through Program capstones or milestones	Program capstones and/or milestones are either non existent or do not match the learning objectives outlined in the program's intention	Program capstones or milestones have relevance to the program intentions but do not state explicit agreed upon competencies that can be measured	Program or capstone milestones have relevance to the program intention with NASM standards applied, but does not have a system implemented to qualitatively track progress	Program or capstone milestones have relevance to the program intention with NASM standards applied and has implemented a system to track student learning from pre-acceptance to final capstone event
Alignment	There is no clear relationship between the outcomes and the curriculum that students' experiences.	Students appear to be given reasonable opportunities to develop the outcome in the required curriculum	The curriculum is designed to provide opportunities for students to learn and to develop increasing sophistication with respect to each outcome. This design may be summarized in a curriculum map.	Pedagogy, grading, the curriculum, relevant student support services, and co-curriculum are explicitly and intentionally aligned with each outcome. Curriculum map indicates each outcome. Curriculum map indicates increasing levels of proficiency.
Assessment Planning	There is no formal plan for assessing each outcome	The program relies of short term planning, such as selection which outcome(s) to assess in the current year.	The program has a reasonable, multi-year plan that identifies when each outcome will be assessed. The plan may explicitly include analysis and implementation of improvements.	The program has a fully-articulated, sustainable, multi-year assessment plan that describes when and how each outcome will be assessed and how improvements based on findings will be implemented. The plan is routinely examined and revised, as needed.

The Student Experience	Students know little or nothing about the overall outcomes of the program. Communication of outcomes to students, e.g. in syllabi, catalog, is inconsistent or nonexistent.	Students have some knowledge of program outcomes. Communication is occasional and informal, left to individual faculty or advisors.	Students have a good grasp of program outcomes. They may use them to guide their own learning. Outcomes are included in most syllabi and are readily available in the catalog, on the web page, and elsewhere.	Students are well acquainted with program outcomes and may participate in creation and use of rubrics. They are skilled at self-assessing in relation to the outcomes and levels of performance. Program policy calls for inclusion of outcomes in all course syllabi, and the are readily available in other programs

Lessons Learned, Changes Made, and Accomplishments

Below the school level the Conservatory is divided into program areas that segregate more specific curricula for each program. In the Music Studies department, the programs are divided by major:
Music Studies:

- Music Therapy
- Composition
- Music Management
- Music History
- Jazz Studies
- Music Education

The Music Performance Department is divided into specific instruments and in some cases instrumental groups:

- Woodwinds, Brass, and Percussion
- Strings
- Voice
- Jazz Studies
- Piano

The process of developing the Conservatory's assessment system has revealed a high level of curricular interdependence. Musicians have always known this; what is unique to the Conservatory, and for that matter the pursuit of music as a career more generally, is that all students need to acquire a minimum level of competency in courses from both the study of and performance of music in order to achieve the learning outcomes we have established for them. Each performance major must reach a minimum level of competency in several music studies courses, and conversely each major in a music studies major must reach a minimum level of competency in the performance area. Jazz Studies, because of its emphasis on both performance AND composition elements, resides in both the music studies and the performance units. A great deal of collaboration and communication across the faculty will be required in order to better understand student learning and to continue to refine out assessment system.

Our process, however, has already yielded positive results. The Music Management program is employing its set of outcomes to assess comprehensive progress in a capstone project, and an assessment project in the core curriculum has identified areas for improvement and refinement for the delivery of introductory musicianship skills. Most importantly, careful planning and consultation is yielding good outcomes and the basis for a sustainable system.

Conclusion and Summary

The Conservatory as a whole is in the beginning phases of the systematic assessment of student learning. The foundation that has been built, however, has influenced and benefitted ongoing efforts to revise curricula, develop our self-study for affirmation of accreditation with NASM, and align with institutional-level assessment and strategic planning. Over time, we will be able to draw upon data to inform teaching and make curricular decisions. And we have not compromised our most important values: that students develop as individuals, and that we understand that development through the lens of our own expertise as musicians.

Chapter 12: Where To Go for More Information

This last chapter of *Assessment in Creative Disciplines: Quantifying and Qualifying the Aesthetic* provides a list of conferences, periodicals, websites, and further reference materials to help you on your journey of exploration of ways to quantify and qualify the aesthetic.

While we have done our best to include what is out there, as of autumn 2013 when this book was turned into the publisher, we acknowledge that our lists are probably not complete and that new conferences are organized and tried and repeated or become "one-ofs", new periodicals pop up in academic circles and old ones go out of circulation, and websites occasionally go defunct. We have provided some basic commentary for each listing to help you choose which is best for your needs.

Conferences

The Arts in Society-- http://artsinsociety.com/ This conference has been an annual event since 2004, and it brings people from all over the world from all areas of the arts community together in face-to-face and virtual format. The Arts is Society is a knowledge community that sponsors the conference, journals, newsletters, and a book publishing venture.

Assessment in the Arts Conference—For both K-12 and higher education faculty and administrators, this conference at Rocky Mountain College of Art and Design features presentations around an annual chosen theme, in addition to being about assessment in the arts. http://www.rmcad.edu/event/2013-assessment-arts-conference-spectrum-possibilities

Assessment Institute at IUPUI—This annual conference, started by Trudy Banta, is held every October in Indianapolis, Indiana. While its focus is on all kind of assessment, some speakers, including the authors of this book, have led session on arts assessment. http://www.assessmentinstitute.iupui.edu/index.shtml

Association of Arts Administration Educators—According to their website, www.artsadministration.org/, "AAAE's annual conferences provide an invaluable opportunity to connect with peers from around the world, share insights, and explore the larger issues of arts and cultural management education. Conferences are hosted by AAAE members in different locations each year, providing an additional opportunity to explore the culture and climate of new places." The 2014 conference will be in Montreal, Quebec.

Association for Theatre in Higher Education—Founded in 1986 as a professional membership organization for individuals and groups (faculty, administrators, students, and theatre practitioners), this association organizes an annual conference somewhere in the United States (2014's is in Phoenix), and the conference focus is entirely on all aspects of theatre arts education. www.athe.org

Athens Institute for Education and Research (ATINER) was established in 1995 to be a forum where academics and researchers from all over the world could meet and exchange ideas about their work. The Institute is headquartered in Athens, Greece, and since its founding, has organized more than 200 conferences and published close to 150 books. They sponsor an Annual International Conference on Visual and Performing Arts at the beginning of June in Athens. http://www.atiner.gr/

ICFAD or the International Council of Fine Arts Deans has an annual conference and triennial symposiums where their members explore "the many aspects the arts in higher education play in offering cultural experiences to the greater community; how we develop and sustain creative communities; and, the important role the arts perform in linking the arts, culture, commerce and the community. Professional development sessions provide participants with new ideas and techniques for a wide variety of programs," according to their website at http://www.icfad.org.

International Design Education Conference—This conference, organized by the Industrial Designers Society of America focuses solely on design education, from K-12 through Ph.D., including assessment and eLearning. The 2013 conference was held in Oslo, Norway. http://www.idsa.org/international-design-education-conference

National Arts Education Association (NAEA) Convention claims to be the only arts education convention of its kind with "over 1,000 participatory workshops, panels, seminars for job-alike groups . . . research reports, discussions, exhibits, and tours . . . keynote addresses by world-acclaimed educators, artists, researchers, and scholars . . . with the opportunity to connect with your colleagues from all over the world," according to their website http://www.arteducators.org/ Members include arts educators from all types of institutions as well as students.

National Association of Schools of Art and Design (NASAD) has been the United States' national accreditor of art and design schools, colleges, and universities since 1944. Their annual October meeting contains professional development workshops and forums. http://nasad.arts-accredit.org/

Sister organization to NASAD, National Association of Schools of Music (NASM) has been the United States' national accreditor of music schools, colleges, and universities since 1927. Their annual November meeting contains professional development workshops and forums. http://nasm.arts-accredit.org/

Periodicals

Art Education Journal is the official journal of the National Art Education Association, and covers a diverse range of topics dealing with subjects of professional interest to art educators.

Arts and Humanities in Higher Education, published by Sage Journals, is an international, peer-reviewed publication that covers everything from arts entrepreneurship and internships to curriculum reform and assessment practices to interdisciplinary art forms.

International Journal of Art & Design Education is a publication of the National Society for Education in Art and Design (NSEAD; U.K.-based) and Wiley. This journal covers all areas of arts and design education, including assessment.

International Journal of Arts Education is published by The Arts In Society and includes articles on e-learning, learner-centered pedagogy, and ways creative arts develop critical thinking, among other subjects.

International Journal of Education & the Arts (IJEA) serves as an open-access platform for scholarly dialogue. "The journal primarily publishes peer reviewed research-based field studies including, among others, aesthetics, art theory, music education, visual arts education, media education, drama education, dance education, education in literature, and narrative and holistic integrated studies that cross or transcend these fields," according to their website.

Music Educators Journal (MEJ) is a peer-reviewed Sage-owned journal that publishes articles about all phases of music education in schools and communities, practical instructional techniques, teaching philosophy, and current issues in music teaching and learning.

Studies in Art Education is a quarterly journal that reports quantitative, qualitative, historical, and philosophical research in art education, including explorations of theory and practice in the areas of art production, art criticism, aesthetics, art history, human development, curriculum and instruction, and assessment.

Articles and Other Writing

Alexandria English Master's thesis on valid and reliable assessment in the arts. http://archives.evergreen.edu/masterstheses/Accession8910MIT/English_AMIT2010.pdf

Assessing Creativity Using the Consensual Assessment Technique, John Baer, Rider University, USA & Sharon S. McKool, Rider University, USA http://users.rider.edu/~baer/BaerMcKool.pdf

Comparative Paper on Painting and Landscape Architecture rubrics. Wolf, K., Connelly M., & Komare A. (2008). A Tale of Two Rubrics: Improving Teaching and Learning Across the Content Areas through Assessment. *The Journal of Effective Teaching*, 8(1), 22-34 http://uncw.edu/cte/et/articles/Vol8_1/Wolf.htm

Northern Illinois University paper on promoting creativity in the art classroom through assessment, www.niu.edu/assessment/committees/CAN/.../ArtEd-CreativityPaper.doc

This article focuses on assessing musical composition and questions whether examiners need more than a single metric to judge creativity in music. http://journals.cambridge.org/action/displayAbstract;jsessionid=2A03F7CD1BDF9211239EC82896929470.journals?fromPage=online&aid=185105

Assessment Plans, Rubrics and Other Tools

Academy of Art general rubric examples
http://faculty.academyart.edu/resource/rubric_examples.html

Assessment Plans and Templates of Vanderbilt University
http://virg.vanderbilt.edu/AssessmentPlans/plan/Designing_an_Assessment_Plan_Samples_and_Templates.aspx

College of Wooster's Assessment Tools and Resources, including rubrics, exit surveys, assessment guidelines, etc.
http://assessment.voices.wooster.edu/general-resources/

Compilation of Assessment Plans in Art and Music from colleges and universities around the country, found on the College of Wooster website:
http://assessment.voices.wooster.edu/disciplines-2/

Digital media rubric, adapted from University of Wisconsin, Stout.
https://www2.uwstout.edu/content/profdev/rubrics/eportfoliorubric.html

Fashion Design competition rubric.
http://www.fcclainc.org/assets/files/Fashion%20Design%202012.pdf

Industrial Design graduate rubric, Academy of Art.
http://gradshowcase.academyart.edu/content/dam/Grad%20Showcase/Schools/In

dustrial%20Design/pdf/ids_mpr_thesis_rubric.pdf

Interior Design competition rubric.
http://www.schools.utah.gov/cte/documents/facs/conference/S08/ID_Moyle_FCCLAInteriorDesignRubric.pdf

Landscape Architecture graduate assessment plan from University of Florida, delineating the tools they use.
http://assessment.aa.ufl.edu/Data/Sites/22/media/2012-13gaap/2012-13-gaap-dcp/3.-aap_grad_landscape-architecture_2012-2013_ver2.pdf

Media and Design Elements rubric, Samford University.
http://www.samford.edu/ctls/archives.aspx?id=2147484107

Metals and Jewelry assessment plan and rubric, Buffalo State.
http://www.buffalostate.edu/design/documents/metals_bfa_assessment.pdf

Rubrics for dance, theatre, music, art at the College of Wooster:
http://www3.wooster.edu/teagle/creativity_rubrics.php

Theatre Arts Department, Utah State: Great assessment plan with assessment methods matrices http://theatre.usu.edu/assessment/assessmentPlan.cfm

Vanderbilt University Best Practices in Assessment Website
http://virg.vanderbilt.edu/AssessmentPlans/Best_Practices.aspx

VATEA Grant Project Rubrics in several creative disciplines.
http://sites.fitnyc.edu/depts/cet/tldocs/SampleRubrics_ArtAndDesignAAS.pdf

Video Project Rubric, University of Wisconsin Stout.
https://www2.uwstout.edu/content/profdev/rubrics/videorubric.html

Vocal Performance Evaluation Rubric, University of Alabama.
http://www.assessment.ua.edu/Rubrics/RUBRIC%20WEBSITE/Marvin%20Latimer.pdf

Winthrop University College of Visual and Performing Arts: Dance and Theatre tools and rubrics.
https://www.winthrop.edu/cvpa/FINEARTS/default.aspx?id=28220

Index

A

accountability 34, 43, 53, 57, 79, 108, 120, 137, 139
Askland 54, 55, 56, 57, 60
Astin 49, 50, 57, 58

B

Bakhshi 122, 126
Ballard 110, 114, 117, 118, 136
Banta 112, 114, 119, 125, 127, 152
Barlow 76, 91
behaviorism 47
Bergquist 98, 105
Blessinger 103, 107
Boone 99, 106, 113, 114, 118
Bosworth 112, 113, 118
Boughton 63, 64, 66, 67
Bregee 5, 10
Bridges 4, 8
Brown 31, 64, 67, 123, 126
Budd xvi, 121, 125, 126
Burnett 108, 113, 118
Buzzetto-More 103

C

Cambridge xvii, 6, 9, 18, 31, 32, 58, 59, 103, 106, 126, 127
Campbell 123, 126
capstone projects 111
Carroll, Lewis 92
case studies 105
change management xvi, 108, 113, 118
charrettes 79, 83
Chase 6, 9
check sheet 74
Chen 6, 10, 22, 47, 58, 106
Ciorba 5, 9
cognitivism 22, 47
Cohen 5, 10, 63, 67
competencies xiv, 38, 75, 76, 80, 83, 95, 149
connectivism 22, 32, 48, 59
connoisseurship model 43, 53, 124
constructivism 21, 22, 27, 28, 29, 30, 31, 32, 47
Contreras-McGavin 6, 7, 9
creativity x, xi, xiv, xv, xvi, 2, 3, 9, 11, 12, 13, 14, 15, 16, 17, 27, 51, 52, 53, 54, 56, 59, 60, 63, 65, 67, 80, 93, 94, 122, 137, 155, 156
Crisp 96, 106
criteria xiii, 2, 4, 5, 6, 8, 12, 34, 52, 56, 57, 65, 67, 69, 71, 72, 100, 101, 102, 103, 112, 122, 148
Cross 4, 9
Cunliffe xiii, xvii, 5, 9, 51, 52, 53, 57, 58
curriculum xv, 35, 36, 43, 45, 46, 47, 49, 50, 62, 63, 66, 67, 72, 74, 79, 84, 90, 96, 110, 111, 115, 123, 126, 138, 139, 142, 145, 146, 147, 148, 149, 151, 154

D

Dawn 103, 106
de la Harpe 6, 9
DeHaan 12, 17

Denecke 109, 118
Dewey 22, 27, 31, 48, 58, 120
Diamond 4, 9
Dionne 13, 17
DiPietro 4, 8
direct assessment 73, 83, 84
Downes 22, 31, 48, 58
Driscoll 4, 7, 9, 136, 140
du Toit 96, 106
Dunn 22, 31, 47, 58

E

Eaton 5, 9
Ehmann 64, 67
Eisner 43, 44, 53, 54, 57, 59, 64, 67, 124, 126
e-portfolios 95, 96, 103, 105, 125
evaluation xiii, 1, 2, 4, 5, 6, 7, 8, 10, 23, 24, 31, 32, 33, 34, 43, 44, 47, 51, 52, 53, 54, 56, 57, 58, 59, 61, 62, 64, 66, 67, 68, 83, 85, 88, 92, 105, 114, 123, 124, 141, 142, 144, 145, 147
Ewell 3, 9, 38, 44, 92, 108, 113, 118
exams 62, 74, 83, 101, 104, 128, 130, 134

F

faculty xi, xii, xiii, xiv, xv, 1, 2, 4, 5, 6, 7, 8, 22, 33, 35, 36, 38, 45, 46, 47, 48, 49, 51, 52, 56, 57, 58, 61, 62, 65, 66, 67, 68, 69, 70, 72, 74, 79, 83, 84, 86, 87, 88, 89, 90, 91, 95, 96, 97, 98, 99, 100, 101, 104, 108, 109, 110, 111, 112, 113, 114, 115, 116, 118, 120, 123, 125, 128, 129, 130, 131, 132, 134, 137, 138, 139, 141, 142, 143, 144, 145, 146, 147, 148, 150, 151, 152, 153, 155
Farmer 123, 126
federal government 1
feedback xiv, 5, 6, 7, 8, 19, 21, 22, 28, 43, 48, 52, 62, 66, 69, 72, 75, 80, 87, 88, 90, 95, 96, 106, 109, 115, 123, 141, 142
Fennel 56, 59

formative assessment 29, 34, 53, 112, 132
Freeman 122, 126
Frey 121, 126

G

Gagne 22, 31, 48, 59
Gardner 73, 80, 92
Gibson 92, 97
Giloi 96, 106
Glasgow 124, 127
Gould 61, 62, 63, 68, 120, 123, 127
group projects 83, 87
Guba 6, 7, 10
Guilford 12, 17

H

Hakel 4, 9
Halpern 4, 9
Hatschek 6, 9
Hawkins 5, 10
Hillier 96, 106
Hitchen 122, 126
Hoey 1, 3, 73, 80, 87, 88, 92, 97, 99, 100, 106, 110, 112, 113, 118
holistic assessment 125
Holland 22, 48, 59
Honig 122, 126
Hope 4, 5, 9, 10
Hume xvi, 121, 122, 125, 126
Hurney 98
Hutchings 108, 114, 118, 119
Hyde 121, 126

I

I-E-O Model 49
implementation 58, 98, 99, 100, 102, 106, 112, 113, 114, 128, 147, 148, 149
indirect assessment 71, 72, 73, 86, 87
institutional learning objectives 146
Itten 45, 46, 59
Ittleson 6, 10

J

Johnson 61, 62, 63, 68, 120, 123, 127
juries 9, 38, 74, 130, 132

K

Kenyon College 86, 92
Kezar 6, 7, 9
Kipling xi, xvii
Kuh 3, 9, 118

L

Latimer 5, 10
Lepi 22, 32, 47, 59
Lewis 13, 17, 69, 121
Light 6, 10, 103, 106
Lincoln 6, 7, 10
Lovett 4, 8

M

Marr 73, 80, 92
Middaugh 112, 119
models of assessment 17, 22, 48, 53
Moore 92, 95
Morman 4, 8

N

Napieralski 123, 126
Nichols xiii, xvii

O

Oakleaf 98, 100, 102, 106
objective assessments 79
online assessment 89, 94, 97, 98, 99, 100, 101, 102, 108
Otis College of Art and Design xvi, 113, 114, 117, 136

P

Palloff 96, 106
Palomba 112, 114, 119, 125, 127
Palumbo 99, 106
Parkes 4, 5, 10
passive assessment 73, 89, 96, 97
pattern recognition 70, 91

Pawlak 98, 105
Penn 5, 10
performance assessments 76
Pillemer 12, 15, 17
Pink xii, xvii, 70, 92
Popova 70, 93
portfolios 2, 6, 9, 10, 38, 72, 74, 103, 104, 106, 124
Portland State University 125
Pratt 96, 106
program review 4, 9, 54, 101, 112, 115, 117, 136
Provezis 112

Q

qualitative 6, 7, 9, 50, 53, 83, 88, 90, 103, 120, 123, 125, 139, 154
quantitative xiii, xiv, 4, 6, 36, 50, 53, 90, 103, 120, 125, 137, 139, 154

R

Raodcy 62
reliability xiii, xv, 3, 6, 79
Rhodes 5, 10, 13, 15, 16, 17
Rice 103, 107
RiCharde 98, 100, 102, 106
Rogers 97, 106, 114, 119
Ross 61, 64, 65, 68
rubrics xv, 5, 6, 10, 43, 44, 55, 64, 69, 76, 83, 84, 111, 113, 114, 115, 124, 137, 147, 148, 150, 155, 156

S

Savannah College of Art and Design xvii
Schein 98, 106
Schute 97
Scott-Kassner 123, 126
Seels 124, 127
simulations 95, 96
Skinner 22, 32, 48, 59
Smith xii, xvii, 5, 9, 64, 66, 68, 118
SNAAP 87
Southampton Solent University 76, 91
standardized assessments 79

Sternberg 5, 10, 12, 15, 16, 17, 21, 32
summative assessment 57, 79
Suskie 4, 10, 48, 59, 93, 112, 119

T

theory xiv, xv, xvi, 2, 15, 16, 18, 20, 22, 24, 27, 28, 30, 45, 47, 48, 49, 50, 51, 57, 58, 59, 95, 104, 111, 127, 129, 139, 147, 154
Tolan 98, 106
Tonski 63, 65, 66, 68
Torrance 12, 17

U

University of Cincinnati xvi, 141, 142, 143
University of Florida 116, 156
University of Nevada Las Vegas xvi, 128
unobtrusive assessment 97

V

validity xiii, xv, 3, 4, 6, 43, 79, 87

value xiii, xiv, xv, xvi, 3, 6, 20, 25, 34, 48, 62, 79, 90, 91, 104, 120, 121, 122, 125, 126, 127, 142, 146
van Nood 103, 107
Volkwein 46, 59
Vygotsky 22, 27, 32, 48, 59

W

Wait 4, 10
Walvoord 4, 10, 112, 119
Wankel 103, 107
Ward xvi, 121, 125, 127
Weiner 4, 10
Wergin 47, 60
Wills 103, 107
Winthrop University 74, 75, 86, 156
Wise 4, 9

Y

Yancey 6, 9
Yorke 123, 127

www.ingramcontent.com/pod-product-compliance
Lightning Source LLC
LaVergne TN
LVHW020331260326
834688LV00037B/978